# backwater

*Nova Scotia's economic decline*

*Peter Moreira*

NIMBUS
PUBLISHING

*In loving memory of my grandparents, Henry Poole MacKeen and Alice Richardson MacKeen*

Nimbus Publishing Limited
PO Box 9166, Halifax, NS B3K 5M8
(902) 455-4286 nimbus.ca

Printed and bound in Canada
Author photo: Marvin Moore

Library and Archives Canada Cataloguing in Publication

Moreira, Peter
Backwater / Peter Moreira.
ISBN 978-1-55109-746-6

1. Nova Scotia—Economic policy. 2. Nova Scotia—Economic conditions—
21st century. 3. Nova Scotia--Social conditions—21st century. 4. Maritime
Provinces—Economic policy. 5. Maritime Provinces—Economic conditions—
21st century. 6. Maritime Provinces—Social conditions—21st century. I. Title.

HC117.M35M67 2009     338.9716     C2009-906117-1

We acknowledge the financial support of the Government of Canada through the Book Publishing Industry Development Program (BPIDP) and the Canada Council, and of the Province of Nova Scotia through the Department of Tourism, Culture and Heritage for our publishing activities.

The Canada Council | Le Conseil des Arts
for the Arts | du Canada

NOVA SCOTIA
Tourism, Culture and Heritage

This book is printed on
ancient forest friendly paper

ANCIENT FOREST
FRIENDLY™

*The power of accurate observation is commonly called cynicism by those who haven't got it.*

— George Bernard Shaw

# contents

# Acknowledgements

*T*his book is the culmination of scores of interviews over a six-year period, and there are simply too many people who have helped to thank them all here. So I will be select, realizing that dozens of people not mentioned here were extremely generous with their time and forthright with their opinions.

First of all, I would like to thank several editors. Patrick Murphy at Nimbus has done a splendid job editing this work, trimming what wasn't needed and honing my arguments. But the book wouldn't have been written if several editors in Canadian publications hadn't first let me report on business events in the region. So I would like to thank Pamela Scott-Crace at *Progress* magazine, Steve Proctor and Dan Leger at the *Chronicle Herald* and John Stackhouse, David Thomas, Doug MacKay, and the editorial staff at the *Globe and Mail*. I'd also like to thank Jane Buss, former executive director at the Writers' Federation of Nova Scotia.

A range of public relations officers has helped me over the years. In particular, I would like to thank the Statistics Canada press office, and the press officers of Communications Nova Scotia. I've criticized the department's growth in this book, but I have always appreciated the professionalism, efficiency, and good humour of the staff.

The following people deserve special thanks for taking the time to discuss economic issues with me: Michael Baker, Victor Boudreau, Wayne Bussey, Charles Cirtwill, Tom Courchene, Tim Curry, Darrell Dexter, Danny Graham, Shawn Graham, Leanne Hachey, Ken Harvey, Ron Heisler, Luciano Lisi, James Lorimer, Stephen Lund, Dan MacDonald, David MacKinnon, Fred Morley, Toon Nagtegaal, Robert Orr, Tim Outhit, Nicole Picot, J. P. Robicheau, John Ross, Brad Smith, Andrew Terris, Dennis Turner, and Mark Whelan.

And finally, I would like to thank Carol, Cat, and Scott for putting up with me while I wrote this book, and I hope, during the next one as well.

# *introduction*

*I* enjoyed a pleasant sense of nostalgia as I headed off to city hall
in Halifax one evening in March 2006 to attend a public hear-
ing into a proposed skyscraper for the downtown. A company called
United Gulf Development Ltd. was proposing to build a $150 mil-
lion, 285-foot-tall hotel and condo project, a twin-tower development
whose curving design would soon earn it the nickname The Twisted
Sisters. The *Globe and Mail*, for whom I often freelanced, had agreed
to let me do a story on the proposal, tying it in with the recent wave
of controversial developments in the city. I'd covered dozens of these
sorts of meetings in the early 1980s, when I was an eager young city
hall reporter for the *Chronicle Herald*. These development stories were
always fun, if a tad predictable: The developer pitches his proposal; the

bureaucracy backs him; the tweedy heritage buffs badmouth the project. And the city council—as often as not—approves it anyway because the city needs the money, and then the whole project gets embroiled in a series of appeals. I was expecting the same sort of deal that night.

But I was in for a few surprises. To start with, the setting had changed. In the early 1980s, there were twelve city councillors meeting in a drab council chamber. There were press tables at the back, and a press room behind them with a few phones and an old couch where you could sleep off a hangover. Since Halifax had amalgamated with Bedford, Dartmouth, and Halifax County in 1996, there were now twenty-three councillors, and the council chamber was enlarged, finished in gleaming oak, and better lit. There were more support staff milling about than I had seen before.

Then there were aspects of the meeting itself that made my jaw drop. Certainly the heritage enthusiasts protested the building. NDP politician Howard Epstein and activist Alan Ruffman—both brilliant orators—summarily trashed the project, mainly because of its height. What surprised me were the young people who addressed the meeting. They had actually taken the time to come out and speak in favour of the proposal—strongly in favour. Years later, I heard that the HRM planning staff was just as gobsmacked by their participation as I was. The first speaker was a mop-topped Dalhousie University student originally from Haiti named Daniel Rossignol. Clad in a sports jacket, he nervously articulated a cogent argument that this development represented a sign of progress in Halifax. "This project is a great stimulant for international students," said Rossignol. "It is a symbol that we are welcome here."

Aaron Murnaghan, twenty-three years old, gave an interview after addressing the council. "For people my age, it is a symbol that this is a progressive city and we can plan to stay here," he said. He paused and added, "I would love to stay here." I spoke to a few students that night who liked the project, and noticed in the next few days that others took the time to write letters to the *Chronicle Herald* supporting the project.

Talking with these post-baby boomers and my own mid-twenties nephews, I developed new insights into how young people view Halifax. The shades of opinion cover the spectrum, but there is a body of thought among this generation that Halifax is an unlikely combination of fun and fusty. The downtown, the bars, Pizza Corner, and the universities— those are all fun. There's also a sense that Halifax—indeed, Nova Scotia—is a rigid fiefdom run by a tight clique that protects its own turf. It's not the people in control pushing for a more open economy here. It's the young people. The last time there was such a battle on generational lines was probably in the sixties—the 1860s, that is.

During the debates of that decade, young, upwardly mobile Haligonians wanted to merge with Canada, and said that old fogies, like Joseph Howe and newspaper publisher William Annand, were clinging to the status quo and trying to torpedo the bold initiative of Confederation. Journalist William McCully charged that it was a battle between men "with fortunes made" and "of fortunes to-be-made." As some of our young people see it, there is a similar dynamic now. The people with entrenched positions are reluctant to allow change. The people without those positions are considering their options elsewhere. They're voting with their WestJet tickets and seeking fortunes in parts west.

That night was an education for me because I knew Nova Scotia's economy was stronger than it was when I was in my twenties. I left Nova Scotia—for what turned out to be a fifteen-year sojourn—in 1988, when the province's economy was supported by declining primary industries, rust belt manufacturers, and deficit spending by govern-ments. The unemployment rate had crested at 14.7 percent in March

1985, but was still stubbornly hovering above 10 percent in 1988. The provincial budgetary deficit would peak at $641 million (according to ratings agencies at the time) in 1993–1994, and the economy was sustained by a federal government spending beyond its means. A money-losing steel mill and money-losing coal mines were among the leading employers in Cape Breton. The bright spots were the fishery, financial companies like Central Trust, and the military.

And boy, did Nova Scotia take a plunge when those economic pillars crumbled. From afar—Ottawa, Hong Kong, South Korea, London—I kept tabs on what was happening at home. Like a volley of punches from a welterweight, economic reality hammered Nova Scotia repeatedly and quickly throughout the 1990s. First, in July 1992, Fisheries Minister John Crosbie shut down the northern cod fishery for what was then expected to be two years, and announced an eight-hundred-million-dollar relief and retraining package for twenty thousand fishermen and plant workers in Newfoundland and Nova Scotia. Fred Morley, then an economist with the Atlantic Provinces Economic Council, said he could not think of a region so devastated since the 1930s dust bowl on the Canadian prairies. The cod stocks still have not returned.

Two years later, Premier John Savage began to tackle the province's dire fiscal situation by imposing an unpopular austerity program. His government cut civil service salaries above $25,000 by 3 percent and reduced health care and other programs to trim government expenditures by $101.6 million. Savage, more than any other premier, deserves the credit for balancing Nova Scotia's operating budget. This fiscal drag on the economy took place as the federal government was implementing Finance Minister Paul Martin's hell-or-high-water restraint program. Some economists believe Nova Scotia got whacked harder than other provinces by Martin's belt-tightening because of the prevalence of military spending in the province and the high proportion of Bluenosers collecting employment insurance cheques.

The next shoe to drop was the 2000 closure of the Sydney Steel Corporation, or Sysco, which had been gradually downsizing since the province took it over in 1969. The government had been trying for eight years to sell the mill, which employed about seven hundred people at the time of the closure. It had lost six billion dollars over thirty years.

In May 2001, the federally owned Cape Breton Development Corporation, known as Devco, closed the last coal mine in Cape Breton, having shut down other collieries over the previous number of years. In all, the federal Crown corporation laid off or retired about 1,500 workers after losing a total of about $1.8 billion over thirty years. By 2009, there was a chance one mine would be reopened by a private operator.

Topping off all these economic earthquakes were several high-profile bankruptcies from companies that should have symbolized the New Nova Scotia. Halifax-based Central Trust had grown into the fourth-largest trust company in Canada with seventeen billion dollars in assets before petering out amid multi-billion-dollar losses in the early 1990s. Knowledge House Inc., a Halifax educational software maker, was feted as a technological up-and-comer, earning a place on the 2001 Deloitte and Touche Canadian Technology Fast 50 list. But the company collapsed in a cloud of accusations and litigation that same year. Cochran Communications Inc. boasted worldwide sales of books and videos based on its character Theodore Tugboat, but the company went bankrupt in 2002 with about nine to ten million dollars in unpaid bills. In the bankruptcy action, federal officers were forced to seize a replica of Theodore that chugged about in Halifax Harbour. And even Peninsula Farm, a successful yogurt-maker in Lunenburg, had to close in 2002 after the Canadian Food Inspection Agency did not approve the pasteurization process used by the company.

So you would have thought I was condemned to a socio-economic Siberia when I returned to Nova Scotia with my young family in 2003. In fact, the place was in pretty good shape—balanced operating budgets, falling unemployment, optimistic business community. In the preceding two years, Nova Scotia had actually outperformed the Canadian economy in terms of GDP growth. I couldn't quite figure out what had happened. Certainly a big factor was the development of the Sable Offshore Energy Project led by ExxonMobil Canada, which has estimated reserves of eighty-five billion square metres of gas to be pumped through the New England Maritime Pipeline to New England markets.

But that was just part of the story. What was more important was an entrepreneurial spirit that had been missing in the 1980s. As a freelance journalist, I was soon writing stories on the new businesses in Nova Scotia that were replacing the likes of Sysco, Devco, and National Sea Products Ltd. as the creators of jobs and wealth in Nova Scotia. When he was Opposition leader, Stephen Harper once said that Atlantic Canada has to overcome its "culture of defeat," but I found little defeatism in the Nova Scotia business community. Remarkable companies were sprouting up.

For *Progress* magazine, I reported on such intriguing enterprises as John Risley's Ocean Nutrition Canada Ltd., which produces a flavourless food supplement with Omega-3, the fatty oil found in salmon and other fish that helps to prevent cardiovascular diseases. The Dartmouth-based company is now the world's leading producer of the supplement, which can be added to just about any food. A start-up called ImmunoVaccine Technologies—which had been founded by a Dalhousie scientist devising birth control for seals—had developed a cocktail of adjuvants and oils that releases drugs slowly. This delivery system, if it is approved, will mean that cancer patients can reduce the number of times they need to take medication. And a Halifax company called Keltic Petrochemical Inc. is planning to build a $4.5 billion petrochemical plant in Goldboro, Guysborough County, creating five to six hundred full-time jobs. Assuming it can find a supply of gas, the plant is to include a liquefied natural gas facility, a co-generation power plant, a steam facility, and a petrochemical plant that will convert natural gas into plastic resins, an essential component in plastics manufacturing.

There are brilliant energy projects. Glace Bay–based Cape Breton Explorations Ltd. is addressing the unreliability of wind power by combining a wind and hydro project. The company is installing forty-four wind turbines and a hydro turbine near Lake Uist in southern Cape Breton. The water from a reservoir near the lake will drive the hydro turbines, but because there is not enough water to guarantee a steady flow, when there's enough wind, the windmills will produce electricity to power pumps to thrust water back up to the lake to drive the hydro turbines again. It's a project profound in its simplicity and environmental brilliance. The company is now diversifying into biomass projects and is intrigued by wave-action power generation.

The project I find most exciting is tidal power in the Bay of Fundy. The world's highest tides—that Joseph Howe liked to boast about in the nineteenth century—could conceivably power a substantial energy industry in the twenty-first. Or they could amount to nothing at all. One thing that is fascinating about tidal power is that the technology is so new, so innovative, that no one knows whether it will produce electricity, how much it might produce, how much it might cost, or what the ecological impact would be. But if tidal power can work, the Bay of Fundy will be one of the best sites on the continent for it. A 2007 report by the Electric Power Research Institute in Palo Alto, California, identified seven sites in North America that might be suitable for tidal power, estimating that in total they could probably support 551 turbines, each producing 1 megawatt of power. Of that total, 250 would be in the Minas Pass in Nova Scotia and 66 at Head Harbour in New Brunswick. That's right—57 percent of the North American tidal power potential identified by the Californians is found in the Bay of Fundy.

Tidal power is just part of a cluster of energy projects whose epicentre is Saint John, New Brunswick, and which is already benefiting the Nova Scotia economy. Irving Oil Ltd. and the Spanish energy giant Repsol YPF SA have constructed their $750-million Canaport LNG terminal, which will vaporize liquefied natural gas and ship it to the New England market. Transporting this gas will be the $350-million Brunswick Pipeline, which is being built by Halifax-based Emera Inc., the parent company of Nova Scotia Power Inc. New Brunswick Power, the provincial government-owned electricity utility, is refurbishing its 635-megawatt Point Lepreau nuclear power plant to the tune of $1.4 billion, a project due to be completed in 2009. And a group of companies, including Atomic Energy Canada Ltd., is studying the feasibility of a second nuclear reactor at the site with a capacity of 1,085 megawatts and a price tag of about $4 billion. If it goes ahead, the reactor could be producing electricity for the New England market by 2016. Tim Curry, president of the Atlantica Centre for Energy, said that if the project proceeds, New Brunswick could be producing a total of 4,400 megawatts of electricity within a decade.

In addition to these developments by local corporations, large companies from outside the region have been coming to Nova Scotia, lured by the wealth of young talent. The most significant was Research in Motion Ltd., which decided in November 2005 to establish a $230-million technical support office in Halifax, creating about 1,250 jobs. Within a year, five offshore financial companies agreed to set up Halifax offices, with promises to create about 1,000 jobs.

And yet, and yet. And yet young people aren't staying in Nova Scotia to reap the benefits. Of course, Nova Scotian diaspora is nothing new. It's part of our heritage. After all, our unofficial anthem is "Farewell to Nova Scotia." The term "goin' down the road" is universally understood to refer to a Maritimer going west to find work, and it is so ingrained in our culture that filmmaker Donald Shebib chose it as the title of his 1970 film about two Cape Bretoners trying to find work in Toronto. But the trend of the past decade is something different. Globalization has created an unprecedented portability of labour. Before the economic crash of 2008, people were migrating to major business centres that offered clusters in a given field, such as finance in Toronto, biotech in Montreal, and of course, the Alberta oil patch, which seemed to have an insatiable thirst for healthy young workers. The statistics show clearly that Nova Scotia is becoming a smaller and smaller part of Canada. The recent recession may have slowed the process, but the long-term trend is frightening.

The latest census shows that there were 913,462 Nova Scotians in 2006, a 0.5 percent increase from the 909,282 people living here ten years earlier. That's a growth rate of 0.04 percent. That stagnant performance was mirrored in other Maritime provinces—down 1 percent to 729,997 in New Brunswick and also down 1 percent to 135,851 in Prince Edward Island. What's important to note is in that same decade-long period, Canada's population grew 9.5 percent, so the Maritimes shrank as a proportion of the Canadian population. If that's not bad enough, we're shrinking as a proportion of the Canadian economy. In the five years prior to 2008, Nova Scotia's gross domestic product rose by 8.0 percent, or at an annual rate of less than 1.6 percent. Meanwhile, the New Brunswick economy grew by a total of 6.7 percent (or 1.3 percent each year), and P.E.I. grew by more than 10 percent in that period, or more than 2 percent annually. But even P.E.I.'s surprising economic growth far underperforms the overall performance for Canada. Canada's GDP rose 12.8 percent in that time, despite the hard times in Ontario and the recent recession. That's an annual increase of more than 2.4 percent—twice the Nova Scotian level. We're living through an unprecedented emigration of our young people, who seem unimpressed with the cleanup of so many economic messes in the 1990s. The Maritime region, for all its charm, offers young people a small jurisdiction with a population and economy that are shrinking in comparison to the rest of the country and continent.

Though I'd started out being rather optimistic about the province's prospects in 2003, the deeper I dug the more problems I found. Compared with the rest of Canada (not to mention the rest of the developed world) our taxes are high, we're burdened with debt, we have a small and fragmented economy, and we're far too reliant on the government. I began to realize the outlook was bleak, and set about writing a book to say so.

Along the way, three things happened that have shaped the finished product, and I will deal with them in reverse chronological order. The third of these three things is that the New Democratic Party formed a majority government in the election of June 9, 2009. That changed the complexion of this project because one of its central tenets is that the Progressive Conservative government did a dreadful job of managing the economy. (It seems most voters drew a similar conclusion.) As the election drew near, I began to worry that the book would lose some of its bite, because I would no longer be criticizing a government in power. Yet, looking forward, I feel no more confident about the prospects for

Nova Scotia with Darrell Dexter at the helm. That's not a slight against the premier—I think he's an outstanding fellow. But the problems facing Nova Scotia are so daunting that I think he and his party will be hard pressed to solve them. I hope this book will show how we arrived at this problem and suggest a path that might improve our economic prospects.

The second thing that happened was the global economic meltdown. It was devastating—utterly beyond most economists' expectations. The global economy contracted, unemployment soared, and corporate profits and house prices plunged. Financial institutions required trillions of dollars of support from governments and U.S. automakers imploded. Here in the Maritimes, we weathered the storm pretty well. The preliminary figures from Statistics Canada show that the province's gross domestic product rose 2 percent in 2008—four times the national rate of 0.5 percent. New Brunswick produced no growth while P.E.I. logged a growth rate of 0.9 percent.

Former premier Rodney MacDonald chose to react to the recession with a stimulus program that will add $1 billion of debt to the $11 billion mountain of debt we're already suffering under. That means the problems I discuss in the coming chapters are virtually all exacerbated. What's going to harm the Nova Scotia economy in the long term is the policy response to the recession, as the extra debt is a burden we can't handle. One other note about the recession is that it threw a lot of statistics out of whack. Statistics are devilish things at the best of times, and I'm amazed at how often I can find different numbers for the same item. But once the recession hit, a lot of the numbers and trends went screwy. So when I delve into data in the coming chapters, I will often qualify my statements by basing them on what was happening before the recession. The downturn will eventually end, and all the forces that were driving young people from Nova Scotia will resume. This book

aims to look at the long-term prospects for Nova Scotia and its two clos-
est neighbours, so I want to base my arguments on long-term trends that
were taking place in an environment of normal global growth. Many of
the phenomena restricting our economic success—the rising Canadian
dollar, high energy prices, the fragmented nature of our economy, our
aging population—will be just as significant as before.

Even before the recession, I had to change my outlook to meet the
demands of my editor and others I spoke to about the project. I wanted
to write about the errors in Nova Scotia policy and our bleak future,
and they all correctly told me I had half an idea. It was fine to point
out all the problems, but the work was incomplete unless I proposed
viable solutions. No one wants to be told something's broken—they
want to be shown how to fix it. But coming up with a solution to Nova
Scotia's problems is a prickly matter. I've made an earnest attempt,
detailing my scheme in the second and eighth chapters. I'm not going
to pretend that it's authoritative or that I have any special qualifications. We live in a province where the government and public agencies
habitually pay consultants six- and seven-figure sums to produce these
sorts of ruminations. I subscribe to the view that a consultant is a guy
who charges you a hundred thousand dollars to tell you what you
already know. So I don't feel any less qualified than a lot of so-called
experts. My qualifications are more than thirty years of journalism in
four countries, covering business, economics and politics, and a deep
love of this region.

Here in a nutshell is the conclusion that I will put forward in the
following chapters: With an aging work force and stagnant population,
and given the high expenses and taxes and limited opportunity, we're
going to have a hard time attracting people. Meanwhile, our standard of
living is threatened because of our massive debt and pressure from other

provinces to change the equalization system. The only solution to these problems is to significantly exceed the economic growth of the rest of Canada. But we won't be able to do that because of a preponderance of government and the rigid fragmentation of our regional economy. Our success is being thwarted by suspicions and jealousies between the provinces, regions, counties, towns, and cities. The best solution—the only solution—for these problems is for Nova Scotia, New Brunswick, and Prince Edward Island to work together to reduce and decentralize the government and end regional trade barriers. We need to adopt policies that seem revolutionary here but are commonplace in other parts of the world. In essence, it's a move to the right of the ideological spectrum—a move, I should note, that has already begun in New Brunswick. I prefer to repackage it and call it a policy of moderation and consolidation. Consolidation is self-explanatory, but I should explain moderation. In several (if not most) economic measurements or metrics, the Maritimes are at the extremes compared with the rest of Canada or the developed world. Nova Scotia has to aim to be in the middle of the pack. That's not an extreme policy; it's moderate. It's bringing us in line with our compatriots. The problem is that many of our current policies are so out of whack with the rest of the country that even a moderate solution seems extreme. Without even this moderate solution, Nova Scotia is in serious danger of becoming an economic backwater.

# *the vision thing*

## chapter one

*A* few years ago, I had an economics column hidden in the belly of the *Chronicle Herald*'s business section, and one week I wrote a column that earned me even more derision than usual. It called for Maritime union. It's a concept I still believe in because it's sheer idiocy that Canada's three poorest and under-populated provinces are competing with one another, imposing different rules, building up expensive bureaucracies. I still hope that one day these three provinces will merge, for Maritime union is a concept that makes so much sense that it has repeatedly resurfaced throughout our history. Sadly, petty suspicions in the region are so strong that the idea never develops into action.

The most famous airing of the Maritime union debate came in 1864 when the Fathers of Confederation met at Charlottetown, supposedly to discuss the merger of the three Maritime provinces. Arthur Gordon, the Governor General of New Brunswick, came up with the regional scheme, largely because he thought New Brunswick was too small a domain for his substantial sense of self-importance. The three Maritime premiers of the day—Charles Tupper of Nova Scotia, Leonard Tilley of New Brunswick, and John Hamilton Gray of P.E.I.— convened at Charlottetown on August 31, 1864, accompanied by their respective opposition leaders. The thinking was that the discussions at Charlottetown would be so momentous that any resolution would need broad support in the provincial legislatures, so the opposition had better be present. The Maritimers were tepid in their support of regional union, but the scheme was not altogether dismissed at this point. Even the great anti-confederate Joseph Howe had told an audience two weeks earlier, "Why should union not be brought about? Was it because we wish to live and die in our own insignificance?" On September 1, a delegation of Canadians led by John A. Macdonald arrived at Charlottetown, and the discussions moved on to a broader confederation. The Canadians were better prepared. They had studies and presentations and the semi-engaged Maritimers lost sight of their regional objective.

Even within Confederation, the Maritime provinces have dabbled with the thought of Maritime union. Precisely one century after the Charlottetown Conference, the subject was broached again at a con-stitutional conference held on the Island to celebrate the centenary. Again the suggestion emanated from New Brunswick. Donald Savoie recounts in his book *Visiting Grandchildren: Economic Development in the Maritimes* that premier Louis Robichaud proposed at the conference that the four Atlantic provinces should consider merging, reducing the number of Canadian provinces from ten to seven. "Should that occur, the focal point of progress and activity would unquestionably and rapidly take a marked shift to the east," he told delegates. Newfoundland wanted no part of it, and Prince Edward Island was reluctant to sign up. Nova Scotia's Robert Stanfield mustered just enough enthusiasm to team up with Robichaud to commission a study of a Nova Scotia–New Brunswick amalgamation.

P.E.I. soon signed up to the proposal as well, and economist John Deutsch was asked to head the group studying the issue. The media backed the Maritime union proposal, as did two-thirds of Maritimers in a public opinion poll. Yet the Deutsch study of 1970 fell short of advocating full union in the short term. Savoie says that while full union was obviously the long-term goal of the group, it initially advocated a gradual move toward union. (Almost forty years later, there has been virtually no increase in co-operation between the provinces, so the recommendation has been ignored.) Why the gradualism? Because, the report said, there were too many groups and individuals too wedded to the current provincial structures. "It can be expected that various influential groups, the holders of franchises and concessions, the bureaucratic apparatus, and many who have vested interests in the existing arrangements would be apprehensive of changes that might bring uncertainties," read the report. "There is no question that in the Maritimes many of these forces weigh heavily in the direction of the status quo."

The bureaucratic apparatus and vested interests stood in the way of Maritime union in the 1970s. That is a shame. And I'm tempted to sound a call for Maritime union now. As I wrote this book, I kept having a vision of the legislature of the unified Maritime Province holding its first sitting on September 1, 2014, in Charlottetown—precisely 150 years after the Fathers of Confederation met there. I spoke to other people about it. And with the exception of Savoie, they looked at me like I had three heads, all of them empty. Either it doesn't make sense economically because the cost savings simply wouldn't be realized, they argued, or broad swaths of the population would feel vulnerable under such a plan. New Brunswick Acadians, in particular, would feel their hard-won gains within the provincial power structure would be jeopardized, and Cape Bretoners and Prince Edward Islanders would worry about being dominated by the more populous mainland. I should have realized the problem with this grand scheme when I was interviewing Premier Graham in his office in Fredericton in February 2008 for a profile in *Progress*. Graham is a charming man, and as our interview ended I decided to ask him about Maritime union. He paused and gave me a blank stare. The charm didn't vanish, but it abated slightly. His response was to the point: "Maritime union," he said, "is a non-starter for a politician."

As I spell out a vision for the Maritimes, I feel I should defer to people like Graham who point out the flaws in my chosen model. Graham, after all, has come up with his own vision for New Brunswick and got himself elected on it, so let's use him as a starting point. When he was still Opposition leader, Graham began to draw odd glances by talking about a weird concept—self-sufficiency. By the time he became premier in 2006, he had defined what he meant and fleshed out a plan for his province: he wanted New Brunswick to be off equalization payments completely by 2026. He got his caucus and cabinet on board, and before long the business community was talking about whether various infrastructure or energy projects would help to bring about the premier's goal of self-sufficiency. Graham did a superb job of rallying New Brunswickers behind him in identifying a target and gaining a consensus that the province needs to wean itself off equalization payments. He also realizes it will be no mean feat to accomplish the task. "I realize we're going to have to punch way above our weight," said Graham with one of his customary laughs.

I should note that this interview took place in early 2008, when Graham's program was still in its warm and fuzzy stage. A few months earlier, he'd appointed a committee of businesspeople to study how to implement his self-sufficiency program. It came back to him with a range of recommendations so vague they were meaningless, from improving education and health care to increasing the population to developing resources and "Put[ting] citizens and businesses first in the delivery of public services." In early 2009, Graham put his own stamp on the program. He and his finance department lowered corporate and personal income taxes, created two personal tax bands, and shrank operating budgets while increasing capital budgets. While public service unions howled, the business community and conservative commentators applauded heartily. The message was clear: to abolish its dependence on equalization, New Brunswick would have to lower taxes, reduce government, and let the private sector grow.

## Equalization

Before I examine Graham's program and explain how it affects the argument I'm constructing here, we should pause and examine what equalization payments are and how they affect life in the Maritimes. The equalization program came into being in the late 1950s as a means of ensuring that all provinces had the ability to pay for the same basic services for their citizens. Based on an arcane concept known as "fiscal capacity," the government uses a formula to determine which provinces are "have-not" provinces, and these provinces receive money to allow them to provide essential services similar to what's available elsewhere. I don't know if it is stated anywhere, but there is always an implicit understanding that each have-not province draws on the program until it's on its feet, at which time it can contribute to the pot and help other provinces. But all three Maritime provinces have drawn on the equalization fund each year in my lifetime, and the payments have become a structural part of the government finances. The governments of both Nova Scotia and New Brunswick drew 23 percent of their revenue from equalization payments in 2008–2009. Nova Scotia's equalization tally amounted to $1.46 billion compared to revenue of $6.27 billion, while New Brunswick's was $1.44 billion of $6.29 billion each year. Prince Edward Island, meanwhile, booked $321.5 million in equalization payments in 2008–2009, or about 43 percent of its $771.9 million revenue stream. Note that these figures comprise only equalization payments and not payments from other federal programs that are given to the provincial governments.

So equalization payments, in round numbers, account for almost one-quarter of every dollar raised by the Maritime governments. And that's a situation that has helped neither Canada nor its Maritime provinces. It hasn't helped Canada because it's money that could be devoted to programs that help all Canadians, and it has created resentment among the provinces that don't receive equalization cheques. The Maritimes haven't benefited because after a half century of receiving equalization payments we are still poorer than Canadians in most other regions. Our median family income is about 13 percent below the Canadian average, and the four Atlantic provinces claim the lowest four places in median income among the Canadian provinces. And finally, there's something unseemly about the way we Maritimers accept this money, year after year, decade after decade. To say it is unethical is too strong a term, but I think it is fair to say it's amoral. We've been accepting these payments for generations, and on a simple moral basis we should be devising a way out of the situation. Graham's plan to wean his province off equalization payments is absolutely the right course to follow, but it will not be an easy plan to implement.

Maritimers often view money from Ottawa as a gift from heaven, but we have jeopardized our economy by generating so much of our government revenue from the equalization system. The alternative would be to generate these revenues from sources within our own jurisdiction, mainly through personal income tax, sales tax, and business taxes, which would mean increasing the number and size of private businesses. As businesses grow and people strive to increase their income, those taxes would grow and the local economy would expand. If we get money from Ottawa, through equalization payments or other means, the only way to replenish it is to ask for more next year. That's a vicious circle that Graham hopes to end in his province.

When I wrote my article on Graham in 2008, I wanted to calculate just how difficult it would be for New Brunswick to eradicate equalization. I did a few rough calculations, running them by a few knowledgeable observers to make sure I wasn't too off base. And when you look at the numbers and place them against the background of New Brunswick's economic, political, and demographic reality, Graham's task looks daunting indeed. Part of the Graham plan calls for the province to add 100,000 people to its current population of 730,000. That's ambitious in itself because New Brunswick's population, like Nova Scotia's, has not been growing for five years. It will require 1 percent annual population growth each year to meet that target by 2026. Meanwhile, the province will also have to increase its GDP by 3.5 to 4 percent every year. That will be difficult, too, as New Brunswick's GDP—again like Nova Scotia's—has been growing closer to the 2 percent range for most of this decade.

That was the outlook in the spring of 2008. Since then, a rather nasty recession has cropped up. The most recent statistics from StatsCan showed New Brunswick's GDP grew by 1.7 percent in 2007 and experienced absolutely no growth at all in 2008, so it looks like Graham will fall short of his goal, unless economic growth accelerates drastically because of his reforms.

But there are more dynamics at play than simply the slowdown in New Brunswick. The recession has bit the hardest in Ontario, the largest economy in Canada, and that means a drain on the entire equalization system. Ontario is so large that if it becomes a recipient of equalization payments, it leaves a lot less money for other provinces. Maybe New Brunswick will be weaning itself off equalization payments more quickly than Graham suspects. Maybe all have-not provinces will.

But what is noteworthy about Graham is that he has opted for something other than the status quo. In the spring of 2009, and to loud applause from the business community and catcalls from the unions, he reinforced his vision with a bold tax plan that cut corporate and personal taxes. I find it riveting to see a politician who challenges his citizens to achieve a difficult task, and to meet a Maritime leader who wants to take less money from the rest of Canada. What's utterly disappointing is that Graham has spurred no copycats in Nova Scotia or Prince Edward Island. No provincial politician in either place has stood up and said, "We have to wean ourselves off equalization." While New Brunswick was reducing taxes, Nova Scotia premier Rodney MacDonald reacted to the recession with a public works package that drew heavily on federal spending.

The whole idea of a public sector stimulus as envisaged by British economist John Maynard Keynes was that it would create demand in times of need, then tail off as the economy recovered. Nova Scotia politicians and bureaucrats head to Ottawa looking for money with the instinctual fervour of salmon swimming upstream to spawn. They can't help doing it. They've done it in the recent past to finance port initiatives, highway construction, sewage disposal systems, health care programs, and a bid for the Commonwealth Games. Journalist Dan Leger, an Ottawa veteran who is now editorial director for the *Chronicle Herald*, has written that federal bureaucrats say they never see representatives from Nova Scotia unless they're approaching cap in hand. The most refreshing aspect of Graham's plan is he wants to devise a program within his province to reduce dependency on the rest of Canada. Other Canadians agree that have-not provinces need less equalization, and they might not be waiting until 2026 to sort it out.

The problem is Canadians west of Quebec don't like sending money east of Ontario in an endless stream. We Maritimers have to realize that Ontario in particular has changed over the years and is still changing. It is a shock to the system that Ontario is drawing on the pool of equalization payments because its manufacturing base has eroded so severely, its GDP growth is lagging the national average, and it has a higher-than-average unemployment rate. Despite these problems, premier Dalton McGuinty appears safe in his job in part because he's found an issue with legs: an unfair distribution of federal money. His complaint that Ontarians paid $21 billion more to Ottawa than they received in services in 2007–2008 was disputed by some, but it struck a chord with his electorate. Even though Ontario is now receiving equalization payments, McGuinty is campaigning to abolish the equalization system. "To speak of have and have-not provinces in 2008 makes no sense," he said in a May 2008 speech to the Ottawa chamber of commerce. "We're a nation of haves these days." What Maritimers may not realize is that McGuinty enjoys considerable support from rank-and-file Ontarians on this issue.

One Ontarian who supports him wholeheartedly is David MacKinnon, a Prince Edward Island native and former official in the Nova Scotia department of finance. Now an Ontario resident, MacKinnon headed an Ontario Chamber of Commerce committee examining regional economic policies in Canada. And he has become a crusader against regional economic policies that he believes are unfair and damaging. He puts forward a coherent message that Atlantic Canada is using its equalization payments to build up a mountainous bureaucracy and offer levels of social programs that often exceed what's available in the so-called "have" provinces.

MacKinnon wants Ontario to form an alliance with Alberta, demand changes to the equalization system, and explain to their electorates why the changes are needed. "Ontario political leaders—federal and provincial—have a strategic choice," says MacKinnon. "They can continue to support federal regional subsidies that have been disastrous for this province, dangerous for others, and that both impede Canada's performance and corrode its fabric...Alternatively, they can recognize that the problem I've summarized is like an iceberg—a much bigger problem than it appears on the surface."

In 2006 MacKinnon delivering a speech in Halifax to a small group that included grimacing bureaucrats from the provincial finance department. When the question-and-answer session opened, someone asked MacKinnon a superb question: Did he plan to deliver his anti-regional subsidies speech in Quebec? One problem with the opponents of equalization programs is they get a tad chicken-livered on the subject of Quebec. Any party aspiring to form a national government needs Quebec because there are only two proven formulae for winning majority governments: a Quebec–Western Canada coalition (Mulroney) or a Quebec–Ontario coalition (Trudeau and Chrétien). Even people like MacKinnon like to highlight the money taken by Manitoba and the Atlantic provinces, conveniently ignoring the fact that of the $14.47 billion paid in equalization in 2008–2009, some $8.03 billion, or 57 percent, went to Quebec. MacKinnon tends to be more strident about the

Maritimes than Quebec, and when Stephen Harper and Jim Flaherty want to pick a fight on equalization, they choose Atlantic Canada rather than Quebec. Quebec will always be politically powerful, and Maritime Canada right now is a scattering of small, divisible jurisdictions.

Most importantly, the equalization system could be renegotiated soon, and other federal funding programs are due to be reviewed in the not-too-distant future. Tom Courchene, a political scientist at Queen's University, said in an interview that a drastic spike in energy prices— among other factors—has changed the relative wealth of provinces, and it's time to review how the equalization system works, and perhaps even depoliticize it. Perhaps, he said, the federal government should look to a system like Australia's, in which a commission of experts decides how much each state should receive.

What no one can say is how Nova Scotia would be affected if there was a review. The federal government is running a huge deficit, and Ontario has a weaker economy than it did previously. I see no reason to believe Nova Scotia is going to receive more money than it has in the past. And equalization payments are just one source of funding that affects the province's income statement. In 2012–2013, Ottawa is due to renegotiate the renewal of the federal-province agreement on health care funding, which distributed $41 billion in funds to the provinces. It was negotiated when Ottawa had a massive surplus. Now it has a huge deficit. Maybe the federal government will maintain the funding levels, but I see no reason to be optimistic.

While I'm in a gloomy mood, I should mention another threat to our way of life. In considering a plan for the future of the Maritimes, we should envisage the worst and ask what would happen if Quebec broke away from the rest of Canada. When you consider that 49.4 percent of Quebecers—and 60 percent of Francophone Quebecers—voted for sovereignty in 1995, it's amazing that Atlantic Canada has not debated more fully what would happen to us if Quebec did separate. Obviously we would be divided geographically from the rest of Canada. That would be a minor problem really, because Quebec would have to negotiate free trade agreements with Canada and the U.S. to survive, so there would still be a reasonably free transportation of goods. The worrying aspect is the political gulf we would face with the rest of Canada. If Quebec leaves Canada, the ideologically conservative voters in the West would gain more power within Confederation. They would be too powerful to ignore. It would leave only a minority of provinces in favour of the equalization system, so that system would likely be done away with within a few years of Quebec's separation. We could lose the system that pays for one-quarter of all our social programs, and our interests would be defended by four puny provinces with a poor record of working together.

So here is what a plan for the Maritimes must do. The most important thing such a plan must do is end our reliance on equalization payments and other federal transfers because we cannot plan on them continuing in their current form. To kick our equalization addiction, we will have to increase our GDP each year faster than the rest of Canada, and do so for a long period of time. And we will have to establish an economic environment that draws people to the region. That's really our mission statement—end the need for equalization payments, improve economic growth, and bolster our political standing. One point I will return to repeatedly is that it won't be enough for us simply to reach the Canadian average in terms of economic growth. We are now lagging the rest of Canada in several areas so to achieve parity with the rest of the country we will need to increase our economic growth at a greater rate than the rest of the country.

I used to think that Maritime union would solve our problems. I figured if we ended the fragmentation of our economy and achieved economies of scale in government, we could lower taxes and all would be right with the world. Now, I'm starting to think the problem with Maritime union is that it would not be an economic program, so the debate would be unfocussed and as various interest groups began making demands we'd probably end up with more government than we now have. Certainly, the amalgamation of the Halifax Regional Municipality produced such a dog's breakfast that it's difficult to believe an interprovincial merger would fare better.

My plan will focus as tightly as possible on economics. It will propose a smaller government and more robust private sector, emphasizing the industrial segments that will grow the most quickly. I hope it will be environmentally sustainable. It will not be politically chic. I will admit that I am completely out of step with the trendy view of economic development often broadcast in the local media. There's a broad swath of opinion that says the key to our economic future is the development of green electricity and locally grown food. I will deal with the development of renewable electricity later, and it could be a key economic development in coming years. But the "buy local" movement is both the wrong economic policy to pursue, and even if it were the right policy, would be insufficient to make a big economic impact. We have to expand our markets, not restrict them to a system of local buyers patronizing local producers. All players would be better served if our producers targeted as large a market as possible. A "buy-local" campaign is essentially protectionist, and for the sake of the world's poorest nations we need less agricultural protectionism, not more. Finally, agriculture is simply too small a part of our economy to merit the attention it gets as a potential economic engine. According to figures from the Nova Scotia government, agriculture, forestry, fishing, and hunting all together accounted for 2.6 percent of the Nova Scotia economy from 2002–2007—down half a percentage point from the previous five-year period. I find that an absolutely astonishing statistic. These former pillars of our economy now account for just over one-fortieth of all we produce. We could double their output, and it still wouldn't amount to much in terms of economic growth. We have to focus on industries that will do more for our economy.

Essentially, I will argue for a complete modernization of the Maritime economy, so the work begun by the Graham government in New Brunswick will spread to the other two provinces and then intensify. The thesis will call for less government and a greater transformation to the information economy. It will demand an integration of the Maritime economy and a more open attitude to exports, especially with the U.S. It will argue that Halifax must be allowed to grow as the commercial hub of the region, but that in return the city must surrender some of its public sector functions to outlying areas. It will call for an end of the parochial, self-interested views that are driving young people to other provinces.

# *labour force*

## chapter two

*O*ne of the more interesting business associations in Nova Scotia is NovaKnowledge, which promotes the "knowledge economy." The idea is that we should be focusing on the parts of the economy that are growing most quickly, whether they are in cultural, technological, environmental, or administrative fields, rather than protecting troubled industries. NovaKnowledge's mission is a noble one (though the organization often falls short of focusing on that singular goal), for it makes sense that Nova Scotia should capitalize on the highest concentration of universities in Canada to develop profitable, sustainable businesses. Like most business groups in the region, NovaKnowledge tends to combine the job of critic and cheerleader—to point out where we need to improve things but to insist we're making progress.

So my jaw dropped when I read the following excerpt from its 2006 annual report card on our progress in the knowledge economy:

> Nova Scotia is facing a labour force crisis. The Baby Boomer generation is on the edge of retirement, and when this wave of workers leaves the workforce, there will be a voracious appetite for new, skilled, and innovative workers. That appetite, at present, cannot be satisfied. There are simply not enough young people in the province to fill these jobs, and there are not enough immigrants to make up the difference.

Crisis. That's NovaKnowledge's word, not mine. This group that I've just accused of having a rose-tinted world view is saying our workforce is facing a crisis, which is defined as "an unstable situation of extreme danger or difficulty."

In an interview in 2007, I asked NovaKnowledge CEO Tim Outhit if the word "crisis" was tossed out lightly and he shook his head. The demographics and studies from various groups all suggest we're heading for trouble with the labour force. And NovaKnowledge is not alone. No serious observer denies that we'll have problems in the future finding the workers our society needs. Leanne Hachey, the Atlantic Canada vice-president of the Canadian Federation of Independent Businesses, says the region is headed for "a demographic tidal wave." Atlantic Canada is facing a more acute problem than other parts of Canada, she said, because we have a smaller percentage of young people in their twenties and thirties. Noted Fred Morley, chief economist of the Greater Halifax Partnership: "If anything, we're underestimating the labour shortages in some sectors."

The subject of demographics drew an expansive response from premier Darrell Dexter when I interviewed him in the summer of 2009. Let me set the scene: The premier had been sworn in only three weeks before, and when I met him in his office overlooking Province House, he looked exhausted. I've known Dexter casually for twenty-five years, and he's a far more lively man (and gifted athlete) than his public demeanour would indicate. On this day, he looked worn down. He had spent almost a month being briefed by the government's senior civil servants so he could grasp what issues faced each department and what resources he had to work with. He and his cabinet were in the early stages of preparing policy, so as you might expect, he was guarded in his answers. But he came to life a bit when I asked him about the coming demographic crunch. He smiled and gestured to his communications director sitting in on the interview. "People around here laugh because I refer to it as the demographic juggernaut," he said.

Dexter noted that by 2026 about one-quarter of the people in Nova Scotia will be sixty-five years old or older, and it makes you wonder who will support them. What's more, only 40 percent of Nova Scotians have a pension (in the private sector, the figure falls to 25 percent) so we will be "graduating this class of seniors into income insecurity and that will be a challenge for all levels of government." In other words, we're on track to have a lot of poor old people. Dexter then added that the governments that are going to be hardest pressed to deal with this are the municipalities, and especially the rural municipalities, because their young people are leaving for cities and their revenue bases are crumbling. With his government in its infancy, Dexter said something had to be done to encourage young people to stay in the province. We have natural resources and we have a strong university base, he said, and what links those two is that they could be the staples for a new wave of entrepreneurship that could convince young people opportunity exists here. "That to me is the single biggest challenge we have in this province—to inspire people to stay," he said.

Crisis. Tidal wave. Juggernaut. Everyone has their own apocalyptic term for the prospects of a stagnant and aging population. The wording differs but it's easy to see a consensus has developed: we're in deep demographic trouble. The main problem is the stagnation of our population, though it is by no means the only difficulty. According to Statistics Canada, Nova Scotia had 938,300 people as of July 1, 2008, a 0.1 percent decrease from five years earlier. If I'd taken the stats from a year earlier, there would have been a 0.7 percent increase over five years. For all intents and purposes, our population is stagnant—neither growing nor shrinking. That means Nova Scotia is becoming a smaller part of Canada. The country overall had a population growth rate of 4.3 percent in that five-year period to July 1, 2008. This has political as well as economic consequences because with each passing generation Nova Scotia—and indeed, the Maritimes—has a weaker voice within Confederation, and the ability to shape national debate is steadily eroding. As Dalhousie University professor emeritus J. D. McNiven points out in his paper, "The Developing Workforce Problem: Confronting Canadian Labour Shortages in the Coming Decades," our population is on track to shrink 4.6 percent to 895,000 by 2026, assuming there are no changes in such factors as government policy, migration trends, or fertility rates.

Even metro Halifax, the fastest-growing place in the province, could only muster growth of 3.8 percent in the five years to the most recent full census in 2006. That not only underperformed the country overall, it also fell well short of the five-year growth rate of 6.9 percent for Canadian cities. And in some rural parts of the province, people are clearing out with a frightening abandon. It should come as no surprise that the Sydney area, with the death of the steel and coal industries, suffered a 3.5 percent fall in population between 2001 and 2006. But what is shocking is that Lunenburg, with a diversified economy including tourism, fisheries, and technology, reported a population decline of 9.8 percent. Antigonish—home to St. Francis Xavier University, perennially rated one of the top universities in the country—had 10.9 percent fewer residents in 2006 than it had five years earlier. Part of the explanation is people moving to neighbouring boroughs, but it's disheartening to think that these two gems in Nova Scotia's collection of towns have had their populations decline so severely in five years.

The statistics hold true for the entire Maritime region. As of July 1, 2008, New Brunswick had a population of 747,300, a decrease of 2,100 people, or 0.3 percent, from five years earlier. For Prince Edward Island, the tally was 139,800, an increase of 1.5 percent. The statistics are quite clear: The Maritimes have had zero growth in this five-year period while Canada has grown by more than 5 percent. To reiterate, we are becoming a smaller, less influential part of Canada. Of course there has been some talk of Maritimers meandering home during the recession because the East Coast has weathered the storm pretty well. The media reported it, but as of writing this book, there was no statistical change in the population of Nova Scotia or P.E.I. in the most recent StatsCan population surveys, and only a mild increase for New Brunswick.

But do these numbers alone make a crisis? Not exactly. The crisis comes when we look at the demographic makeup of our stagnant population base. The 2006 census showed that 15.1 percent of Nova Scotians were 65 or older, the second-highest level in Canada, and up from 13.9 percent in 2001. (Saskatchewan's 2006 level was the highest at 15.4 percent.) The other Maritime provinces had the same problem

—14.7 and 14.9 percent for New Brunswick and P.E.I., respectively, both up more than one percentage point in the five-year period. The overall level in Canada is 13.7 percent. This is the point at which the problem becomes a crisis.

According to Statistics Canada figures as recited by McNiven, there are now about 128,000 Nova Scotians aged 65 or over, and that number is going to climb about 70 percent to 218,000 by 2026. That 70 percent growth rate pretty well mirrors the growth of senior citizens across the country. What is worrying is what's forecast to happen with Nova Scotians still working for a living. The number of 15- to 65-year-olds in Canada is estimated to rise marginally by 2026. But in Nova Scotia, the 15-to-65-year-old bracket will fall drastically, from about 638,000 to about 558,000. McNiven adds that the participation rate in the labour force is due to drop to 56 percent from 63 percent by 2026. In short, we are projected to have fewer young people supporting a lot more senior citizens.

Look at it another way: There are now almost five people in the 16-to-64-year-old bracket—the people who are producing goods and services and generating growth—for every senior citizen. Within a decade and a half, that ratio is expected to fall to just over 2.5-to-1. The best guess now is that within a quarter century, Nova Scotia will halve the number of income-producing adults in relation to its number of retirees. The prospect of every two-and-a-half people supporting a retiree is bleak indeed, especially given rising medical costs.

But remember that the soaring cost of health care is only one of the difficulties faced in the mission to provide medical services to citizens. There is also the problem of finding the right people to provide those services, a larger problem than ever before with the current labour crunch. A January 2008 report on Nova Scotia's health care system by consultants Corpus Sanchez predicts a shortage of five hundred registered nurses in the province by 2010. "If human resources are not addressed, other strains on the system become moot, as without health-care professionals and health-care workers in general, there can be no system at all," said the report. That is a prediction for 2010. What about 2020? Or 2030? Come to think about it, will we be able to attract teachers in the future, or police officers, or tradespeople to build and maintain hospitals and schools?

## Avoiding the Demographic Crisis

The dire labour outlook across the Maritimes is affecting our way of life on two fronts. First, before the recession, businesses had trouble finding staff, and that impeded their ability to grow, which suppressed economic growth. Certainly the demand for staff receded during the recession, but a tight labour market promises to be a problem again as the world economy recovers. Beyond the economic consequences, labour shortages are also restricting the government's ability to provide the services we all demand. Those problems will no doubt intensify in the coming decades as the workforce ages, simultaneously creating demand for health and social workers and depriving the workforce of able-bodied workers. How do we fix such a cataclysmic problem? So far, the Maritime provinces have sought to increase population by two policies—first, by working with the federal government to guide immigrants to the province, and second, by luring home native sons and daughters who have defected to other parts of Canada.

The immigration programs are the most structured part of this strategy, as each province has signed Immigrant Nominee Program agreements with the federal government, which direct a certain number of immigrants to each province each year. Nova Scotia, for example, set up an Office of Immigration in 2005, now costing five million dollars a year, with the goal of encouraging more immigrants to settle and stay here. The department has two targets: first, it aims to attract 3,600 immigrants annually by 2010; and second, it aims for a 70 percent retention rate in the period from 2006 to 2011. (The retention rate in 2005 was 40 percent.) That 3,600-person target is within the realm of possibility, as Nova Scotia attracted about 3,700 immigrants in 1995, or 1.7 percent of the Canadian total—though that took place before a 10-year immigrant drought. To be fair, former premiers John Hamm and Rodney MacDonald deserve more credit than they've received for the leadership they've shown on immigration. Maritimers had always been suspicious of "come-from-aways," convinced they were here to steal somebody's job. Hamm and MacDonald made great strides in convincing people that we have to be more accommodating to people coming to the province. This can still be a difficult place to break into socially and professionally, and there are still institutional barriers to entering the workforce here (just ask a teacher who's come from another province). But there's been great progress in making the Maritimes a more open society, and the two Tory premiers deserve credit in Nova Scotia.

Nova Scotia's effort to attract immigrants has come with some controversy. The Nova Scotia Nominee Program, in place between 2001 and 2006, created a scandal that roiled the government of Rodney MacDonald. Under the program, immigrants paid $130,500 in exchange for a six-month work term with a Nova Scotia business. (The program was administered by a private company, Cornwallis Financial Corporation, which was awarded the contract without a public tender.) But after hundreds of immigrants said they were not given jobs in their area of expertise and were left with little for their investment, the province agreed in 2007 to repay $100,000 to six hundred immigrants.

About two hundred additional immigrants believed they were owed money by the province but received nothing. The scandal received blanket coverage from the media, but it has been resolved and won't have a lasting impact. But that doesn't mean the immigration program doesn't still have problems. Even if Nova Scotia makes its immigrant targets and the administrative costs don't rise at all, the province will be paying about $1,400 for each immigrant it attracts, which seems like a steep price. I should add that plenty of people in the Nova Scotia business community consider it money well spent because they view immigration as the most pressing need facing the province.

Let's come at the problem from another angle. Let's say the Nova Scotia government does meet its short-term targets on immigration. Suppose the province starts adding 3,600 immigrants annually, and every single one of them is in the 16-to-64-year-old age group and at work. (That is incredibly optimistic, as some of these immigrants will be seniors, children, or stay-at-home parents. Historically, each working immigrant moving to Nova Scotia brings 1.2 dependents.) And let's say that 70 percent of them stay in Nova Scotia (even more optimistic). If all those overly optimistic factors are met, 58,000 people would be added to the Nova Scotia workforce by 2030. If that were to happen, the number of people in that 16-to-64 age bracket would still drop by about 40,000 from the current level, and the ratio of working-age people to seniors would still drop to 2.8-to-1 from 5-to-1. J. D. McNiven estimates Nova Scotia would have to attract about 14,300 immigrants per year—almost four times the current target—for eighteen consecutive years and have all of them remain here to rely on immigration to solve our labour shortfall. Obviously, if the immigration policy is going to work, it is either going to have to accelerate dramatically, be part of a broader program, or both.

But those 58,000 people would represent a slice of the population rapidly accruing wealth, right? After all, study after study has shown that immigrants to Canada outperform people born here in terms of wealth creation. That was once the case, but more recent studies have found things have changed. Immigrants are no longer the engine for wealth they once were. In the 1970s, it took an average immigrant ten years to reach or exceed the income levels of his or her Canadian-born peer. But that trend began to change a generation ago. By the end of the 1980s, a male immigrant who'd been working in Canada for ten years was earning 90.1 percent of what his native-born neighbour was making. By the end of the 1990s, that figure had deteriorated to 79.8 percent. There's no sign of improvement yet. This suggests that relying on immigrants for population growth means there's a risk the result will be a growing proportion of the population with less earning power, therefore less ability to generate economic growth and pay taxes. A close examination of the demographics suggests that immigration will not be enough to solve labour problems nor to create the wealth needed to grow the economy.

The programs to lure home wayward Maritimers have been more sporadic than the immigration program, and focused mainly on convincing people raised and/or educated in the Maritimes that the region offers more opportunity than they may have realized. These initiatives highlight the growing financial services sector, the Research in Motion operation in Bedford, and the development of the energy hub in southern New Brunswick. Sometimes, Maritime governments hold trade shows targeting specific careers, as Prince Edward Island has done to promote nursing careers on the Island. The four Atlantic provinces have even worked together, such as in December 2006 when they co-operated with the region's private sector to pay for a forty-page glossy newspaper supplement in Calgary, advertising career opportunities on the East Coast.

Some expatriates have returned—I'm one of them. It's impossible to say how many have come back, though there are indications that the eastward flow has increased during the recession. But you'd have to be optimistic to the point of daffiness to believe that this program has proven successful—and the same thing could be said of the immigration initiative. It's not that these programs are bad ideas, or that they won't help in the future. I'm saying that so far there is every reason to be skeptical about their success. The immigration numbers? The retention rate? They don't mean much, really. The sponsorship scandal in the long-run is utterly meaningless. The only things that matter are whether our population is growing and whether the average age is declining. The immigration program began in January 2005, and since then Nova Scotia has spent upwards of fifteen million dollars on immigration and who knows how much on promotional programs to attract other Canadians to the province. In January 2005, Nova Scotia's population was about 938,100, and three-and-one-half years later the population was about 938,300. The number of immigrants coming to the province is not the key statistic to examine; it is the size and age of the population that we should focus on. Maybe there will be a mild improvement in 2009 because Nova Scotia has weathered the recession well, but success will only come when we see our population increasing during good times. As Outhit told me in June 2009, "In a year or two this recession is going to end, but we're still going to have the demographic problems."

Let me put an exclamation point on that: demographic problems in the Maritimes are going to endure for the rest of the baby boomers' lifetimes. This problem will not go away. Every jurisdiction in the developed world will be suffering the same problem, so we will be competing with other jurisdictions for workers. But Atlantic Canada will have a tougher time than other Canadian regions because so much of the post–baby boom generation has already been lost. Any meaningful fix is going to take decades. There are, of course, short-term measures to do more work with the existing population. Productivity has to improve. Right now, we're doing a pretty bad job on that front—improving but still pretty bad.

## Increasing Productivity

Let me begin with one morsel of good news: in the final years of the Tory government, Nova Scotia began to get more out of its workers, and we are catching up to the rest of Canada in this area. In 2008, Nova Scotia recorded a 0.9 percent gain in worker productivity, according to StatsCan, while the productivity in Canada overall fell 0.5 percent. New Brunswick and P.E.I. scored less well, with a respective 0.6 percent decline and 0.2 percent increase. Nova Scotia's gain outpaced every province except Saskatchewan, and it is part of a process of the province slowly closing the gap with the rest of the country. In 2000, Nova Scotia's productivity was 79 percent of the national level, and there had been a minor improvement by 2008 to about 82 percent. So the situation in Nova Scotia is improving, but we're still a long, long way from being where we should be. In fact, only two provinces have lower worker productivity rates than Nova Scotia—New Brunswick and Prince Edward Island. When you consider that we're competing in a global economy, sitting at the bottom of the Canadian barrel is a cause for concern. Data from the Bureau of Labour Statistics in the U.S. ranked thirteen developed countries in terms of productivity, measured by GDP per hour worked, and Canada placed tenth on the list. That performance has not been improving. The same bureau ranked sixteen developed countries on their improvement in productivity from

1995–2005, and Canada placed thirteenth. So Nova Scotia is competing in the global economy, but its productivity is at the bottom end of one of the weaker developed nations.

So what is it with workers in the Maritimes? Is it that employees on the East Coast have a weaker work ethic? It doesn't seem so. In 2006, the average Canadian worker put in 33.9 hours a week at his or her job, while in Nova Scotia the figure was 33.5 hours—a difference of only about 1 percent. Is it because we're too unionized? That assertion collapses at first glance as well. In 2006, 31.7 percent of the Canadian workforce was unionized, while in Nova Scotia the figure was 28.3 percent. So why are we less productive?

"Lack of investment," says NovaKnowledge's Tim Outhit. His theory is that Nova Scotia businesses simply have not invested enough in equipment and technology to allow their workers to work productively. Luckily, this problem is finally being addressed. In the ten years to 2001, there was only one year in which Nova Scotia invested a greater proportion of its GDP in plant and equipment than the national averages for Canada and the U.S. Between 2002 and 2005, however, Nova Scotia has met or exceeded the Canadian figure three of the four years and exceeded the U.S. figure twice. Fred Morley, chief economist of the Greater Halifax Partnership, agrees that investment is the problem. He noted that Nova Scotia exceeds the national average in investment in equipment for financial services, and as a result Halifax has one of the most productive workforces for financial services in the country. To improve productivity, we'll need to attract more investment in assets that improve productivity, and that investment will have to be generated by both the public and private sectors. In other words, the government would do more long-term good by giving corporations tax breaks or low-interest loans for capital investments in equipment or new technology than it would by paving a road. I know—I bellow for the government to pave my road as well. But we need productive investments to make sure our workers produce more in each hour of work.

## Employment Insurance

Another area that needs to be addressed as the world emerges from the recession is employment insurance. I used the passive voice there because the provincial government will likely not be the determining body. As of the summer of 2009, there is a national debate raging about this very topic, and what the Maritime provinces think will probably count for very little. The other provinces and the federal government are making proposals, and we'll likely have to put up with what they decide. All of which is very strange, given that people in other parts of the country consider EI to be an "Atlantic Canadian" issue. Little perpetuates the stigma of the lazy and impoverished Maritimer more than employment insurance. You want proof?

In the federal elections campaigns of both 2000 and 2004, the various incarnations of the Conservative Party accused the Liberals of "pandering" to Atlantic Canada for proposing changes that would make it easier to claim EI. And when the Liberals lost nineteen Atlantic Canadian seats in the 1997 election, several party members blamed the losses on the government's tightening of EI rules a few years earlier as part of Paul Martin's program to slay the budget deficit. There are unemployed people elsewhere in Canada, and they claim EI. But sadly, when EI is mentioned in the rest of the country, our compatriots imagine lazy Easterners as the claimants. Part of the problem is that the only labour category that gets its own rules for EI is fishermen, because of the seasonal nature of that business. But even the fishing industry is facing labour shortages now, and the rules have not changed to reflect the new reality. In Clare in southwest Nova Scotia, for example, the lobster season of 2006 proved difficult because fishing captains and wholesalers couldn't find enough people to sail the boats, check the traps, and sort the lobsters. "On the boats and in the pounds, they were scrambling to find people," Paul-Emile LeBlanc, general manager of the local credit union and former president of the Clare Chamber of Commerce, told the *National Post* in December of that year. "Those employees were no longer here. It was a real eye-opener for people."

Well, here's another eye-opener. Despite all the labour shortages, which even impacted the economy in rural Nova Scotia, EI in the first decade of this century was as much of a crutch for seasonal workers as it had always been. I'm not talking about what happened in the recession, because once the recession hit, there were tragic layoffs and bankruptcies right across the country. But during the good times, when the Canadian economy was firing on almost all cylinders from 2002 to 2007, one of the more disturbing aspects of Nova Scotia's performance is that EI claims did not noticeably drop in the province.

Consider this: In April 2002, there were 427,400 Nova Scotians happily at work, which meant that we had an unemployment rate of 9.8 percent. Not everyone was able to find work, and so there were 44,340 people who were receiving employment insurance benefits. Fast-forward five years. By April 2007, the Nova Scotia economy had generated more than 23,000 new jobs. There were now 450,900 people at work, and the unemployment rate had fallen by almost two full percentage points to 8.0 percent. You would think the number of EI claimants would have fallen. But according to Statistics Canada, the number of people receiving EI cheques in April 2007 had barely changed at all—it was 44,020.

The EI stats fluctuated wildly from month to month, and it seems the number of claims dropped during the winter over the past few years. But the big picture shows that as the unemployment rate fell, just as many people claimed employment insurance as before. At a time when we're facing a labour "crisis," we had just as many people accepting employment insurance as when we had a huge labour glut. By the summer of 2009, the focus of all governments in Canada was on making sure EI flows as quickly as possible and for as long as possible to people who have been laid off in the recession. You won't get any argument from me on employing such a strategy during a downturn. But once the slump is over, you can bet that the federal government and the provinces will move to reform the system. What the Nova Scotia government should do in the debate on these reforms is to go along with what everyone else proposes, which would probably include an end to special provisions for seasonal workers. What it should not do is launch a campaign to preserve the system of seasonal workers using EI as a means to avoid working in the off-season. Such a system is not only unfair to workers who toil all year, it is also harmful to a small economy with a declining workforce.

## The Next Step

Of course, seeking more investment and reforming EI are only partial measures—they do not strike at the heart of the matter, which is that our working population is shrinking and we need more workers. But why are we shrinking in relation to the rest of Canada? The simple answer is a lack of opportunity. We have roughly the same birth rate and life expectancy as the rest of the country, but young people—regardless of their education level—perceive greater opportunity elsewhere. In theory, in May 2009 it was easier to find work in

Nova Scotia or New Brunswick than in Ontario; the two Maritime provinces' unemployment rates were 8.9 and 8.8 percent, respectively, while the Ontario figure was 9.4 percent (P.E.I.'s was 13.1 percent). But Western Canada still offers more and better prospects with provincial unemployment rates ranging from 4.9 to 7.6 percent, and over the long-term it's likely that Ontario's economy will rebound. And not only is it easier to find work in other provinces, but the work usually pays better. Nova Scotia workers on average earned $705.08 a week in February 2009, second-lowest in the country after Prince Edward Island, while in Ontario the figure was $836.34, Alberta $924.01, and British Columbia $790.82. So the young people who go down the road generally find it easier to get a job, and the odds are the job will pay at least 12 percent more than at home.

But the immediate low pay is only part of the problem. Nova Scotia has more citizens in university and community college per capita than any other province in the country, and these students are not spending four years in college because they want to go on to earn seven hundred dollars a week. They want careers, not jobs. They want to go to an organization where they can plan to progress, increasing their earnings and satisfaction as they get older. They want to know if they don't like one company, they can—without moving to another city—switch to another firm with the same opportunities, and then maybe to another company again. They want to know that their spouse will find the same opportunities—a huge factor in attracting people that is too often overlooked. And they want an area in which those opportunities will still exist in thirty years so their children will have the same outlook.

How do I know this? From personal experience. My wife is English and our two children were born in England. When we thought about moving here in 2003, these were the things we considered. You might argue that we're the exception because immigrants in the popular imagination are people from exotic cultures who speak other languages and require settlement programs. But on that matter, popular imagination is quite mistaken. Figures from Statistics Canada show that in any given quarter two of the three largest immigrant groups to Nova Scotia are Americans and Brits. If you include people moving from other parts of Canada, by far the majority of people moving to the Maritimes come from developed, English-speaking countries, and they have economic aspirations we will have to meet. When people move to this region, they have to be impressed enough with the opportunities here that they want to stay. As of 2005, six out of every ten immigrants to Nova Scotia was packing his bags and leaving again within a few years. Ron Heisler, then the head of the province's immigration and settlement division, tried surveying some of the immigrants who left to find out the reason for their departure. "They said Nova Scotians were among the politest people they'd ever met, but without the right jobs, there was no way to make a go of it," Heisler said in a 2005 interview. Immigrants, it turns out, leave for the same reason young Nova Scotians do—because of the lack of opportunities.

So, what should be done?

McNiven concludes we have to adopt a combination of policies, such as attracting immigrants, improving productivity, and encouraging older workers to remain on the job. "These approaches, or a combination of them, would help, but none is a magic solution," he writes. "What is clear, however, is that Canada, and Nova Scotia, cannot afford to do nothing." First, the province should continue with the existing immigration and promotional programs. They're not problematic, just insufficient. The government should also push for reforms in employment insurance that would encourage more people to work.

Many observers advocate drawing on groups with high unemployment levels, such as Aboriginals, African-Nova Scotians, and people with disabilities, to solve labour force shortfalls. Of course we should encourage more employment for these groups because it is the right thing to do. But it is not a cure-all for our labour problems, because these groups make up a small proportion of the overall population. Finally, we have to draw investment to the province to improve productivity and create an environment in which people perceive opportunity—not easily done because investment capital will flow to the jurisdictions where the greatest returns are available. Attracting people will be no cakewalk either; simply telling them there is opportunity here won't work. If people move to the Maritimes and find there is less opportunity than they thought, they will move away again. We need a long-term program that improves the economy, because the only way to create opportunity and attract investment is to ensure our economic growth exceeds that of other provinces. In the ensuing chapters, I hope to demonstrate how that can be done.

# cost of living

## chapter 3

When the Maritime governments began their campaign to lure people back to the East Coast, one of the biggest selling points was the affordability of a comfortable life. They thought our wayward sons and daughters would move back home if they understood how much cheaper it is to live in the East than in Calgary, Toronto, or Vancouver. In announcing its Come to Life ad campaign in 2005, the Nova Scotia government issued a press release stating: "The slogans re-inforce *the fact* that Nova Scotia is a more affordable place to live (italics mine)." And soon there were billboards across Calgary imploring errant Bluenosers to come back and buy a home, or maybe two—a reference to the much cheaper real estate in Nova Scotia. The federal government took a similar line: "The cost of living in Atlantic Canada is 25 percent to 65 percent lower than other major North American regions," trumpeted the Atlantic Canada Opportunities Agency website.

Governments have toned down their claims that the cost of living is low in the Maritimes, but they have not done away with them. The Come to Life website still states: "A low cost of living and a high quality of life make Nova Scotia an enjoyable and affordable place to live." It borders on false advertising. The whole premise is based on the notion that real estate is cheaper in this region than in the largest cities in the country. But when you consider the lower wages, the higher taxes, and the higher household expenses, consumers in the Maritimes have less spending power than Canadians living west of the Maritimes. In other words, if you choose to live on the East Coast, you will likely have less money after you've covered household expenses than if you lived in other parts of Canada. I know this statement goes against the grain, but I think the evidence in the following pages will back it up.

The first thing to keep in mind is that most Maritimers have less money to chuck around than their countrymen elsewhere. As noted in the previous chapter, the hourly wages in the Maritimes are among the lowest in Canada. So the young people who go down the road generally find it easier to get a job, and odds are the job will pay at least 10 percent more than at home. Even in the comparison between metropolitan areas (StatsCan's most recent data is from the 2006 census), Halifax's level is more than 11 percent below that of Toronto or Calgary.

If Maritimers earn less, they also take home less because taxes in Nova Scotia are among the highest in Canada. The sad fact is that most Nova Scotians will pay a higher tax rate than those in most other provinces even though they earn less. Just take a look at the employees I mentioned in the previous paragraph. If an Ontario employee earned $43,472 in 2008—the average wage in that province—he or she would have paid $7,808 in income tax, or an average tax rate of 17.96 percent, according to the LMS Insurance tax calculator. A person earning the same wage in Nova Scotia would have paid $9,468 in taxes for an effective tax rate of 21.76 percent. So if two employees make the same wage in the two provinces, the one in Nova Scotia is going to pay about $1,340 and almost four percentage points more in tax. But the problem with that statement is that the Bluenose employee is unlikely to make as much as the Ontarian. According to StatsCan, the Nova Scotia worker on average would make $36,664. And that person last year would have paid $7,085 in taxes for an effective tax rate of 19.2 percent.

So what does that all mean? Even though the average Nova Scotia worker earns 15.7 percent less than the average worker in Ontario, he or she pays a higher tax rate on those earnings than a similar worker in Ontario. In fact, the Nova Scotian pays almost as much tax in absolute dollar terms as the Ontarian, even though he or she makes almost $7,000 less. The bottom line is that the average after-tax income in Nova Scotia in 2008 was $29,579 a year, or $2,465 a month—17 percent less than the average $35,664 annually or $2,972 monthly take-home pay in Ontario. So if all else is equal, we have on average 83 cents to spend in Nova Scotia for every dollar they have in Ontario. The gap would be lower if you're comparing employees in the major cities of Halifax and Toronto, but there is still a substantial gap.

## Housing

So it's a good thing we get such a bargain on our homes, and by and large, homes in Nova Scotia do cost less than those west of New Brunswick. Statistics compiled by the Canadian Real Estate Association show the average house price in Halifax in May 2009 was $248,209, while the average in Toronto was $395,609, Vancouver $583,674, and Calgary $382,632. The Canadian average was $319,757—well above the headline price in Halifax. But it's worth noting that Halifax home values actually rose during the recession while those in other areas fell. In any case, it's an accepted fact that someone moving from Toronto to Halifax should be able to find a home with the same specifications (and likely much less commuting time) for a saving of more than one-third.

I'd like to calculate what this can mean to the average homeowner. Let's assume a family has a mortgage equivalent to 75 percent of the purchase price of their home, which cost the average price in their market. That would mean that at interest rates on offer in May 2009 (4.19 percent over 25 years) the family would pay a monthly mortgage of $998.49 in Halifax compared with $1,591.45 in Toronto. That means the average family in an average house will pay $592.96 less each month by living in Halifax rather than in Toronto—a saving of about 37 percent. No doubt that six hundred bucks a month is going to help any family.

I will readily admit that this is a huge incentive to move from a big city to Halifax, and the attractions extend beyond the realm of cost savings. Generally speaking, a family can buy a better house—bigger and in a nicer neighbourhood—in Halifax than in Toronto, and this is a key lifestyle factor. A family's house can determine how it lives, how much private space each member has, how it enjoys time together, and how extended family and friends perceive it. A house can affect whether people enjoy visiting that family, determines the family's neighbours and the children's peer group, and is a breadwinner's greatest statement of his or her success in life. It is a family's proverbial castle. The affordability of good houses also means young families can buy in areas near good schools. Finally, an affordable home in Halifax usually comes with far shorter daily commutes than in Toronto, which allows more family time. So in no way am I diminishing the importance of cheap real estate. But it is only one factor, and the issue of cheap property is far more complicated than the sticker price might suggest.

For someone moving from a big Central or Western Canadian city to Nova Scotia, the attraction of cheap real estate can be a trap. In reality, few people move from an average house in Toronto, Vancouver, or Calgary, to an average house in Halifax. The reason to move to the Maritimes is to enjoy a better life than the big Western cities can offer, and that usually means having a nicer house. If you sell that $395,609 bungalow in Toronto, you're probably going to take the equity you built up and sink it into a nicer house in Halifax, and that house is probably going to cost more than $248,209. I've met plenty of people who have moved to the Halifax area from other markets, and I haven't met anyone who has moved down-market during the move. In fact, everyone I can think of moves up-market. So if you're going from a three-bedroom in Toronto to a four-bedroom with an ocean view in Nova Scotia, you're going to surrender a large part of those theoretical savings.

Then we have to remember that most people returning to Nova Scotia have built up equity in their homes in more dynamic housing markets during the real estate boom of the last two decades. That means they are paying a low mortgage compared to the value of their house. Let's assume someone bought a house in Newmarket, Ontario, five years ago for $200,000, of which $150,000 was financed by a mortgage. That house is now worth $300,000 even after the recent property slump, but the owners are still making mortgage payments based on that initial $150,000 mortgage deal. Now they decide to sell in Toronto and move to Halifax. Let's say they move up-market and buy a $375,000 home in Halifax—a nice four-bedroom home on a quiet street on the peninsula. Even though the family is now able to put about $150,000 of equity into their new home, their overall mortgage is going to rise to more than $200,000. This is one of the key problems with saying real estate is cheap in Nova Scotia. A lot of returning come-back-from-aways buy better homes in Nova Scotia than they had elsewhere, and they end up with larger mortgages because their old mortgage was based on property values of several years ago. Even if they have maintained the same income in Nova Scotia that they had elsewhere—a big if—their other costs are going to be significantly higher here than they were used to.

Let's take a look at non-discretionary spending, starting with property tax. Yes, homes are cheaper in Halifax than in Toronto or Calgary, but property taxes in Halifax are astronomical. A homeowner pays a tax rate of 0.8548 percent of the assessed value of a home in Toronto and 0.50 percent in Calgary. In Halifax, the rate is 1.347 percent, almost 60 percent higher than in Toronto and about two-and-a-half times that of Calgary. So even though you may get a bargain buying a house in Halifax compared with Toronto, the tax you pay will probably be about the same, and Nova Scotia property assessors are aggressive in increasing the assessed value of homes (although the increases are capped for now).

## Other Costs

The other costs residents incur by living in Nova Scotia add up quickly. In Calgary or Toronto, homeowners are able to heat their houses with gas, whereas in Halifax they have to use heating oil. (Heritage Gas is now installing gas into homes in peninsular Halifax, but the rollout is slow. What's more, the costs will be more than in other cities because laying pipe is expensive on the peninsula's bedrock and because federal incentives for natural gas pipelines are no longer available.) The relative costs of heating oil and natural gas depend largely on the cost of the commodities themselves, and natural gas prices have tended to be more stable than oil. One study, by Taracen Gas of British Columbia, showed that the average annual household heating cost of gas with a mid-efficiency furnace in 2006 was $758 whereas with heating oil it was $1135. Some experts in the field add that an oil-burning furnace needs $100 to $200 of mainte-nance a year, whereas a gas furnace needs little upkeep. In short, someone heating their home with natural gas—an option unavailable to most Nova Scotians—will save $500 to $600 per year over a heating oil user.

Then there's electricity. According to information provided by Manitoba Hydro, Halifax has the third-highest residential power rates among a list of sixteen Canadian cities, exceeded only by Englehart, Ontario, and Charlottetown. A household using 750 kilowatt hours of electricity a month as of May 1, 2009, has an annual electricity bill of $1,191 in Halifax compared with $1,098 in Toronto, $1,028 in Calgary, and $605 in Vancouver. Admittedly, the gap between power rates in Halifax, Toronto, and Calgary is narrow, but Halifax still exceeds the costs in the other cities. Again, if people have a larger house in Halifax than they had in the other city, they likely need more fuel to heat it and more electricity to power it.

Then we can add on other household expenses that are higher in Nova Scotia than in many other provinces, as anyone driving a car in the vari-ous provinces knows. According to the Calgary consultancy MJ Ervin and Associates Inc., consumers on June 30, 2009, paid $1.00 a litre in Toronto, 95 cents in Calgary, $1.10 in Vancouver, and $1.05 in Halifax. Annualized at forty litres a week, the costs are $2,080 in Toronto, $1,976 in Calgary, $2,288 in Vancouver, and $2,184 in Halifax. So while we don't have the highest gas bills, they are higher than many others.

Trying to definitively compare costs in various cities is a fool's errand because there are too many variables, and each family's costs will dif-fer. But there is strong evidence that many household staples are more expensive in Nova Scotia than elsewhere. Take milk, a staple for young people if ever there was one. According to Statistics Canada, the price of milk in Halifax in the first quarter of 2009 was the fourth-highest in the country, at $1.94 a litre. It was exceeded only by $2.87 per litre in Toronto, $2.59 in Windsor, Ontario, and $2.39 in St. John's. But we pay less than the Canadian average for chicken and cheddar cheese.

Perhaps the best measure of consumer prices in respective cities is Statistics Canada's Market Basket Measure, which assesses what a basket of household goods would cost a family of four in the largest city in each province. The most recent study, for 2006, shows that Halifax ranked fifth for the total costs at $29,073—7.4 percent less expensive than the costliest city, Toronto, and 11.8 percent more expensive than the cheapest city, Regina. Painted in broad brush strokes, Halifax is one of the cheapest cities for transportation, in the middle of the pack for shelter, and more expensive than most for food, clothing, and other expenses. It's not cheaper to live here than elsewhere. The costs of living here are in middle of the Canadian pack, and people who live here pay higher taxes and earn less money than if they lived elsewhere. So after all the bills are paid, Maritimers, on average, probably have less money in their pockets than Central or Western Canadians.

With all statistics, you can dispute little details here and there, but the overall picture is clear. Other than housing, life is at least as expensive in Nova Scotia as in other parts of Canada, and it is especially expensive for low-income families that need such necessities as food, gasoline, heating oil, and electricity regardless of their ability to pay. Other than housing, it's difficult to point to an item or service that is less expensive in the Maritimes than in other provinces. Any claim that life is 25 to 60 percent less expensive than other provinces is pure poppycock cooked up by wishful-thinking bureaucrats. The statistics suggest the cost of living in Halifax is about 7.4 percent less than Toronto. But the federal government's statistics also show that Haligonians earn 11 to 12 percent less than their confreres in Toronto, and pay about four percentage points more in income tax than Torontonians. The conclusion is stark and indisputable: if the average person chooses to live in Halifax (or other parts of the Maritimes) his or her disposable income will shrink.

## A Real-Life Example

In January 2007, I wrote a column for the business section of the *Chronicle Herald* strongly disputing the notion that life in Nova Scotia is cheaper than elsewhere. It cited many of the stats I just listed, though I've updated as many as possible for this book. The column ran on the inside of the business section, and on the day it was published I began to get emails in response, with a strong majority agreeing with me. That afternoon the business editor, Steve Proctor, called to let me know the response was so strong that the paper was setting up a special webpage to highlight the letters. My own inbox received thirty-four emails by the end of the day—all but two agreeing with me. By far the most vocal were the CBFAs—the patriotic Nova Scotians who had lived elsewhere and then come back to the East Coast and found life harder here than in Western and Central Canada.

One respondent was Mark Whalen, a native of Heart's Desire, Newfoundland, who'd missed the East Coast while living in Calgary and decided to take a job in Halifax. Mark, 29, and his wife Kimberley, 35, drove back east in August 2006 with two young children. For seven years, he'd been working at the temporary staffing agency Kelly Services (Canada) Ltd., and now he was being promoted to the branch manager at Kelly's Halifax outlet. The promotion did not come with a raise, because Kelly pays a manager in Halifax the same rate that Mark was earning at a lower level in Calgary. But they had been told—and everybody said it—that the cost of living would be cheaper in Halifax than in Alberta.

Mark and Kimberley had bought a 1,400-square-foot starter home in Calgary in 2001 for $165,000. They put it on the market at just the right time in 2006, and benefited from a bidding war. The home sold for a whopping $325,000. They took some of the windfall to pay off Mark's student loan. Then they decided to buy a 2,000-square-foot home in the modest Middle Sackville area of suburban Halifax for $265,000. They felt they were being responsible with their money, but after cashing out of one of the world's hottest property markets, they thought they could upgrade a bit. Even though their mortgage in Nova Scotia was $10,000 more per year than the mortgage they'd had in Alberta, they were confident in the decision.

Very soon after moving to Nova Scotia, they felt their windfall from the Alberta property market slipping from their grasp. The bills started to roll in, and they were a lot more than Mark and Kimberley were used to. Their property tax had doubled to $2,400 a year from $1,200 a year in Calgary, while their heating bill had tripled to $3,600 a year from $1,200. And they had to meet these additional expenses with a lower income, for two reasons. First, Mark's salary was unchanged but he was paying more taxes in Nova Scotia than he had in Alberta. Second, Kimberley had not found a job that could compare with the job she'd left in Calgary. Previously, she had a managerial position with a retail company, and the payscale for her job classification was about $22 to $23 an hour. In Halifax, she'd discovered, the pay for store managers is about $13 to $14 an hour. After seven months in Nova Scotia, she was still looking for a job that paid an acceptable amount. "We don't know if we can make it here," said Mark Whelan with a sigh in 2007. "If you stay here, you're going to be struggling. Why do the government and our business leaders promote coming back here when you know you're going to be struggling if you come here?" (I tried to contact Mark to update his story, but he has since moved on from Kelly Services.)

It's a good question. But here is a better one: why does the government of Nova Scotia ignore consumers in so many of its policy considerations? The government does provide rebates for consumers on such things as heating oil, and will lobby to hold down power rates when Nova Scotia Power Corporation applies for rate increases. But in so many policy decisions, the government is perfectly content to add to consumers' costs. I'm not talking here about high taxes—I'll deal with those in a later chapter. I'm talking about government policies that make us pay more than necessary to private operators.

## The Bottom Line

Until recently, Nova Scotia was one of the few provinces that required annual vehicle inspections, even on new vehicles. We have to renew our drivers' licences every five years, for no good reason. Nova Scotia regulates gasoline prices, and the government's own study says regulation costs the average motorist $12.50 a year or a total of $6 million. That's the official government estimate, but the Atlantic Institute for Market Studies has an up-to-the-second estimate of what gasoline regulation costs motorists. On July 1, 2009, the third anniversary of the policy taking effect, it had cost us $20.6 million and counting. The New Democratic government plans to retain the policy.

The foolish regulation that really gets up my nose is land migration, as the local bureaucrats have chosen to call it. Basically, this is a program to build up a computerized land database because until recently Nova Scotia was the only province whose land records were printed on paper in regional courthouses. So beginning in 2004, whenever someone sold, subdivided, or refinanced a property, he or she had to pay a lawyer to have the property resurveyed and filed in the new electronic database. (This process is required only once, so the next time a property is sold the so-called migration to the database is not needed.) This system primarily benefits property lawyers, surveyors, and realtors and is entirely financed by local homeowners. Since 2004, my family has sold a cottage and refinanced a mortgage, and we had a really good lawyer recommended to us by our mortgage broker. He charged about $800 a pop for the land migration. Will I ever see that $1,600 again? No way. Will I receive benefits equal to $1,600 for having my land migrated to an electronic database? Nope. Beyond my own selfish rant, there is an economic cost for this policy. About 5,400 homes a year are sold via the multiple listing service in Nova Scotia. Assuming about half of these needed to be migrated, Nova Scotians spent about two million dollars on land migrations when they sold their homes last year (assuming the price I paid—and I think I got a pretty good deal from my lawyer). The total was undoubtedly more than that because there would have also been refinancings, private sales, and commercial properties. This is wasted money for the average consumer.

The bottom line is that Nova Scotians earn less, are taxed more, and then have to pay more for many of life's necessities. That means we have a lower standard of living than other Canadians, can save less, and over time accrue less for our retirement. This may seem like a self-centered, rather shallow argument focusing mainly on our ability to buy things. The first response to that point is we all work hard and we like to afford life's little luxuries. Second, we established in the previous chapter that we are facing a demographic crisis, and we're going to have a hard time attracting or retaining able-bodied workers if they have to make finan-cial sacrifices to live here. If we're going to succeed, we have to reduce the cost of living—even through small measures. But beyond that, there is a clear economic problem with a jurisdiction whose citizens have a hard time accruing wealth. If Nova Scotians earn less and are taxed and charged more than other citizens, then we have less wealth in our society, which means less investment and therefore a weaker economy. Our financial problems will persist in part because the government is not removing inefficiencies like gas regulation from the economy.

So what should the government do? There's not a lot it can do in the short-term, other than phase out the foolish regulations I listed above. It should also work feverishly to set up a harmonized electricity market with New Brunswick, P.E.I. and Newfoundland and Labrador (discussed further in chapter five). In fact, governments should enlarge their internal markets wherever possible, because the more customers Maritimers have for goods and services, the cheaper they will be for everyone. Business leaders have called for the Maritime provinces to adopt a Trade, Investment and Labour Mobility Agreement, or TILMA, such as the one Alberta and British Columbia have signed. That would be a start, because goods and services being traded across a broader market will cost less than those trading in smaller markets. Nova Scotia and New Brunswick took baby steps in this direction in February 2009, when they announced a Partnership Agreement on Regulation and the Economy, which ensured some portability of labour. The move tiptoes in the right direction, but is little more than TILMA-lite. To really expand the Maritimes' internal market, the governments are going to have give it a better shot than that.

All of this raises a question: Why do we live here? Why would we choose to live in a place where we earn less, pay more taxes, and buy things that are more expensive? There are all kinds of reasons to love living in the Maritimes—the simple answer is we like the lifestyle. But there are difficulties here as well, which I will explore in the next chapter.

# quality of life

*chapter four*

*I* used to commute for three hours a day.

For eight years, my family and I lived 130 kilometres north of London. I'd leave the house each morning (except on days I could work at home) at 6:20 AM to catch the 6:40 train to the city. If it was on time (a BIG if), the train would get into King's Cross Station at about 7:30. Five to ten minutes later I would be on the Tube heading into the city. Then I had a short walk to the office. So I would usually be at work by about 7:50, maybe 8:00. The worst part of the commute was the cost—about ten thousand dollars (Canadian) a year at the exchange rates of the day. If we'd been living in London, I could probably have counted on a total daily commute of ninety minutes, maybe more, at an annual cost of about three to four thousand dollars (Canadian).

That wasn't our most outrageous cost in England. No, that would definitely be the private education of our two children, which cost about twenty thousand dollars (Canadian) a year (and would have soared substantially had we not left the U.K. in 2003). But we felt we had to put our kids in private school after our daughter, aged six, complained one day she couldn't hear the teacher in her public school from her seat in the hallway. There was no room for her seat in her crowded classroom. We lived in a decent neighbourhood in a dreary town. The streets were overcrowded with cars. The local river was a revolting olive colour. There were growing racial problems; my sister-in-law, a police officer, was the first person arriving at a racially motivated homicide one night.

I was chatting to a couple of friends one day. We were bitching about life in England, as all Englanders do, and I remember saying longingly, "I have this dream that one day I could live in a place where your surroundings ease stress rather than add to it." They looked at me kind of funny. It was as if they were admitting that such places do exist, but it was beyond the realm of possibility that any of us might escape to one.

My family and I did. We moved to Nova Scotia. I will admit that I don't regret the move. Yes, Nova Scotia has its problems, but it is a great place to live for many reasons. Above all, the people are marvellous, and we've made great friends here. We live and work in St. Margaret's Bay just south of Halifax, which does offer an environment that inspires relaxation rather than stress. It's a peaceful life with a beautiful view. Halifax is a forty-five-minute drive away, and offers a variety of restaurants, basketball games, theatres, cinemas, concerts, and shopping. Manhattan it ain't, but it offers some cultural life. We found, in short, the Nova Scotia quality of life that the provincial government has been advertising.

Over the six years we have lived here I've decided that this definition of "quality of life"—essentially, pleasant and fun—is pretty shallow. An assessment of Nova Scotia lifestyle must address whether Nova Scotians receive the staples of life in the same abundance and at the same cost as people living elsewhere. That means looking at the quality of the infrastructure, of the health care system, of public safety, of the education system, social support systems, arts, and the environment. Finally, we'll have to look at whether these services will be maintained at affordable levels in the future. These are the components of the lifestyle that modern citizens demand. We've established that Nova Scotia—and its neighbours—needs workers to move here, and that the workers will probably earn less money than they would receive elsewhere. If those workers are going to come, they'll need to be assured that they can receive the basic amenities they'd expect elsewhere. It's a difficult task because what I, with two school-age kids, want in social programs is different than what the next guy (maybe facing retirement or with serious health issues) wants. It's even hard to say any particular social program is good or bad, because stats are unreliable.

## Education

I find it impossible, for example, to categorically say whether the Nova Scotia education system should be praised or condemned. There are problems, but overall my family's experience has shown that there are some great schools here with some great teachers in them. Our kids have thrived, largely because they like the environment they're being educated in. Others find it easier to pass judgment on the Nova Scotia schools, and generally speaking they lean toward condemnation, because Nova Scotia performs worse than other Canadian provinces in international aptitude tests.

In December 2007, for example, the Organisation for Economic Co-operation and Development released its Programme for International Student Assessment, a comprehensive survey of fifteen year-olds in fifty-seven countries. In the OECD's rankings, Canada placed sixth in science with 534 points, seventh in reading with 527 points, and ninth in math with 527 points. Not bad. British Columbia, Alberta, Ontario, and Quebec led the country in all these categories, exceeding the national average in almost every one. Nova Scotia, with respective scores of 520, 506, and 505, placed sixth among Canadian provinces in science, seventh in reading and ninth in math. In fact, the Maritime provinces were relegated to the bottom three positions in Canada in every category except one—Nova Scotia scored three more points than Saskatchewan in science for a sixth-place finish. Hurray. In general, the three Maritime provinces are the absolute worst in Canada at preparing our children for higher education. Before we faint from the horror of the scores, we should note that the Maritime provinces handily beat the OECD average in each of these categories, and defeated such economic heavyweights as the U.S., Britain, Germany, France, and Spain. (There are all kinds of these tests and they generally show similar results. There is some quibbling about whether there are signs of improvements, but looking at the big picture they all tell a similar tale.)

Here's one graphic illustration of the problem we have in education. For the past few years, Michelin SA has given tests to each job candidate hoping to work in one of its three factories in Nova Scotia. The failure rate is about 50 percent. The candidates are all high school graduates, but they lack the skills in reading, writing, and mathematics to work in a modern factory. These are skills that should have been mastered by a junior high school student. This failure was so egregious that it caught the attention of the Atlantic Institute for Market Studies, the conservative think tank that has launched a crusade to improve educational results on the East Coast. That's not surprising. What was interesting is that Darrell Dexter was so appalled by this result that the Michelin tests became common fodder for his campaign speeches in the 2009 election. Dexter is on record as saying the province has to improve its educational performance.

Maritime students clearly perform worse than their Canadian peers in basic academics, but I still think this can be a fine place to educate your children. The region offers qualities that are vitally important in a child's upbringing but don't show up in statistics. Obviously, parents who can calculate their daily commute in minutes rather than hours will have more time to spend with their kids. Not everyone has a speedy commute, but a larger proportion of people do here than in other places. That means children tend to get more time with their parents. We are not free of the consumerism that plagues modern society, but we are less obsessed with it than elsewhere. There's also a sense of community that often means we know each other's kids and spend a lot of time with them through sports or youth groups. If the adage is correct and it does take a village to raise a child, then children are raised well in the Maritimes. I have no statistics to back up these claims—there are no stats on consumerism or community spirit. But my experience—and the experience of a lot of people who have lived elsewhere and moved here—suggests that the attitude of Nova Scotians creates a tremendous environment for nurturing young people. So we tend to nurture young people well, but not educate them well. Actually, I'm not even comfortable with that statement. There are some children who are bright, work hard, or both, and they thrive in this system. The problem is our schools continue to move children through the system who quite clearly should be failed. Maybe this is a nationwide problem, but our school system also lacks fundamental discipline, which has to be addressed.

I'd like to offer two pieces of advice, and they might seem to be contradictory. First, the problem is bad enough to suggest that the current structures and culture are insufficient to fix it. The results we're seeing simply aren't good enough, and we will have to change the way we teach children. That will offend certain groups—most likely the school boards, the education department, and the Nova Scotia Teachers Union. My suggestion is they learn to live with it. Taken as a whole, they are failing, and politicians and taxpayers have to collectively tell them that we will not tolerate this failure any longer. My second piece of advice is that we should not hold up test results as the be-all and end-all in education. They are important, yes, but there is a danger that we can fall into the trap of believing that if all students grade at 70 percent or better in the three R's then they have a complete education. Schools in Britain have fallen into that trap. My wife and I found that schools in that country have focussed too narrowly on the results of so-called core subjects, meaning children receive too little exposure to physical education, art, music, even history and geography. It's difficult to produce nice, clean statistics for holistic education. But as Nova Scotia raises its performance levels in literacy, numeracy, and the sciences, it must attain the goal of producing well-rounded students. I will be the first to admit there are no easy ways to do that.

I'm going to limit my suggestions to reforms within the public school system. AIMS has advocated letting parents pull their children out of the public school system, and providing them with a voucher to cover 70 percent of the cost of sending their child to a private school. It would attract investment to education and raise performance levels, says the plan. The theory is that the remaining public schools can then apply more resources to educating the students who remain. My own view is that it's a policy worth considering, but I'm not convinced it would cure the malaise that exists in many public schools. It would be preferable to see the government attack that malaise directly.

I'd prefer that we adopt another proposal advocated by AIMS—do away with the school boards. Do we really need these bodies? Have they proven successful? If you answered yes to either of these questions, please supply evidence, cross-referencing to the OECD study mentioned above. Of course we don't need one school board for every hundred thousand citizens, and our academic results have proven that they are failing our students. We should work on phasing out these school boards. We could have a single provincial education department to oversee the province's schools, which, as the Atlantic Institute for Market Studies likes to point out, means accommodating a smaller population than that covered by the Edmonton School Board. The result would mean more resources channelled into the schools themselves.

I've just suggested stripping out an entire layer of bureaucracy, likely at the loss of hundreds of jobs. Certainly that's an overreaction? Actually, it's not. We're facing a demographic crisis—not a problem, a crisis. We need to attract workers to a province where they will likely have less spending power than in other parts of Canada. If we fail to do that, we will not have the workforce to provide the services and generate the income we will all need as we age. We're now going to tell those newcomers that their children will be fed into what's rated one of the worst school systems in Canada. Part of the problem with the Maritimes right now is we all are content with mediocrity. We need to reform our system and punish bad performance. Everyone agrees that we're facing a demographic crisis, but the government—generally with the backing of the business community—has chosen gentle remedies. Usually, as you will see in coming chapters, they involve building up a larger bureaucracy to address the problem. Wrong choice. With the demographic crisis that we've facing, we have to—absolutely *have* to—streamline government and make it more productive. The school boards have let us down. Let's do away with them and use the savings to hire more teachers and keep the students in school more.

One of the problems with schools in Nova Scotia—and you don't need a PhD in education to figure it out—is kids simply are not in school long enough. In 2007–2008, for example, the Halifax Regional School Board had 195 days of school. But ten of those days—a full two weeks—were either professional service days or system-wide conferences, which means the teachers spend their days in meetings rather than in the classroom. On top of that, there were eight snow days—days in which the weather was so bad that it was considered unsafe to travel to school. The Toronto District School Board, by contrast, cancelled no school because of snowfall in that year, though there were four days in which buses were cancelled because of snow. There were another eight snow days in Halifax in 2008–2009, while school boards like Toronto's and Quebec City's had none. I've checked with contacts in Toronto and Quebec City. They have snow. Even Halifax children with a perfect attendance record spent eighteen days per year—9 percent of the total—at home because of the weather or ridiculous bureaucracy or a combination of the two. Of course there are alternatives. The state of Maine has snow days, but those days are added on to the end of the school year. Here's another suggestion: on snow days, teachers could come to schools in the afternoon (with very rare exceptions, roads are cleared by noon) to attend meetings on professional development or other school functions. Then the next in-service day could be cancelled.

No Nova Scotia school board has tried such a program, assuming that the powerful teachers' union would oppose it. Instead, we're left with a complacent system in which our kids are in school fewer than 180 days per year, preparing to compete in a global economy against Japanese students who spend upwards of 220 days per year in the classroom. As well as the problem of children missing almost one-tenth of their school, there is an economic cost to this practice. A large percentage of the workforce has children, and a lot of people simply can't go to work when their kids aren't in school.

Part of the problem with our schools is simply the unwieldy relationship between the disparate bodies responsible for providing education. The Halifax Regional School Board accommodates almost half the province's students, and has to work with the provincial education department for funding and curriculum. Both bodies must work with the Teachers Union and a network of home and school associations. The elected officials running the board in this decade exacerbated the situation with their tragicomic bickering. One meeting in 2006 was cancelled for lack of a quorum because a group of members walked out to support a colleague who had been removed for missing too many meetings. On another occasion, a member refused to adhere to a seating plan at board meetings, saying it violated his rights under the Charter of Rights and Freedoms to sit where he liked. Early morning radio hosts had a field day talking about the school board, whose behaviour would not be tolerated in any of the classrooms they were responsible for. Then-NDP education critic Bill Estabrooks, a former teacher and principal, described the board as "the laughingstock of staff rooms." Finally, in December 2006, education minister Karen Casey had enough and fired all thirteen elected members. The board members voiced their outrage, then protested just as loudly when the board cancelled their eight-thousand-dollar annual stipend. They actually believed they would still be paid after being fired. A new board has since been elected.

What's discouraging is that no one seems to really be improving things in Nova Scotian schools. The teachers union maintains that non-teaching days are sacrosanct and shouldn't be touched. The biggest school board was until recently a comedy of errors. The only improvement seems to be the introduction of an International Baccalaureate program in public schools, which will give our strongest students an arena in which they can thrive.

## Post-secondary Education

Post-secondary schools are often touted as a highlight of the Nova Scotia economy—which is not to say there is no room for improvement. Two things have changed in the last generation to make this system all the more important. First was the creation of the Nova Scotia Community College system, and second was the premium placed on commercial research and development, which the universities should benefit from. The community college was formed in 1996 when the province amalgamated its disparate collection of technical schools into a single institution with campuses in fifteen towns and cities across the province. This incredible institution, which has an enrolment of twenty-five thousand, will play a key role in Nova Scotia's economic future because it can produce workers—specific types of labourers for the jobs being created by the modern economy. It trains tradespeople, who are badly needed in the new industries developing in the Maritimes. It produces the technicians and artists who are in demand in the knowledge economy, and it does so quickly, training these people in two-year courses, rather than the four-year courses provided by universities.

Of course, Nova Scotia is rightly proud of the fact it has more universities per capita than any other province. From the ivy-lined venerability of Dalhousie, to the spirited joie de vivre of Acadia, to the newfound elitism of St. Francis Xavier, the province has a portfolio of respected universities that draw students from around the world, and the research performed at these institutions is a bona fide engine of economic growth. According to NovaKnowledge, Nova Scotia's private sector research and development amounted to about 0.3 percent of GDP in 2003, which placed it among the four worst performers in Canada. However, with the addition of universities and government, the total rose to 1.4 percent of GDP, which ranked third in Canada behind Ontario and Quebec. ImmunoVaccine, which I mentioned in the introduction, is just one of the companies that have grown out of research performed at a Nova Scotia university that was later commercialized. Such companies are big businesses. In April 2006, the Atlantic Association of Universities and the Atlantic Canada Opportunities Agency jointly commissioned a consultants' study that found the schools are a $4.4-billion-a-year industry, employing 16,665 people for a total payroll of more than $1 billion. Universities are the number one source of immigrants for the province, and our health care is undoubtedly better because so many specialists are attracted here to teach at Dalhousie's medical school.

Can there be any complaints with such a windfall? There are actually two problems—there are too many universities and they're too expensive. Nova Scotia has eleven universities, with eleven presidents, eleven boards, eleven finance departments and eleven registrars and eleven human resources departments and eleven public relations departments. Their recruiters are all competing against one another for a declining number of students.

This is needless duplication, especially when you consider there's a cluster of universities in Halifax, where these services could easily be consolidated. University honchos consistently argue that the separation of universities ensures their individual character and consolidation would save no money. It's an unconvincing argument. Certainly the Nova Scotia Community College vastly improved its cost structure and programs after it became a single institution. Dalhousie, for example, decided in 2008 to offer a bachelor of education program—even though Nova Scotia is already producing three times more teachers than there are available positions each year. These universities could better coordinate course offerings if there were fewer institutions.

What's more, Nova Scotia's universities, at least, need to improve control over their costs. Dalhousie University, the largest, has increased its administrative costs 95.6 percent from 2000–2001 to 2007–2008 to $18.6 million, while total academic spending only rose 51.2 percent. Acadia University recently agreed to a wage package for professors offering a top annual salary of $132,000 per year. As columnist Dan Leger in the *Chronicle Herald* pointed out, this is almost as much as the $148,000 paid to top profs at Berkeley, which has seventeen Nobel Laureates. Six months later, Acadia announced it was cutting back on such discretionary spending as travel, training, advertising, and equipment. So the university is paying excessively high salaries to profs but cutting back on training and equipment. The high salaries wouldn't be such a problem for the overall economy were it not for the fact that the costs are handed on to students. In the days of a knowledge-based economy, Nova Scotians pay more to attain knowledge than any other Canadians.

According to a Statistics Canada report in October 2008, the average undergraduate in Nova Scotia must pay tuition of $5,932 per year. The good news is that figure is 2.9 percent less than the previous year, but the bad news is the 2007–2008 figure is more than 5 percent more than second-place Ontario and 25 percent more than the Canadian average. New Brunswick students averaged $5,590 while on the Island the average tuition was $4,530. The most depressing statistic regarding university tuitions is that in Newfoundland and Labrador, undergraduates pay tuition of $2,632—less than half the Nova Scotia level. Newfoundland has one university, Memorial University. So while Nova Scotia boasts of its eleven universities, Newfoundland contents itself with one, and its students reap the benefits.

In the last chapter, I mentioned that I once received a flood of emails after writing a column in the *Chronicle Herald* on the high costs of living in Nova Scotia. A few of them were from students complaining about the cost of tuitions in Nova Scotia. The comments that particularly struck me came from a few students who would soon graduate and head to Central or Western Canada to get jobs. The high tuitions in Nova Scotia are badly exacerbating the brain drain, they argued, because so many students have to take on debt to pay for school. Young people graduating with twenty to thirty thousand dollars in student loan debt have to go where they can make the most money, and that isn't in Halifax. They have to go West and pay off that debt.

## Health care

The education system is easy to assess in comparison to the health care system, which many Canadians view as the most important service provided by the government. Not only is the health care empire vast and complicated, but good health care involves so many expensive pieces of technology that few of us have the expertise to say what's needed, what's desirable, and what's optional. What we all do know is that health care is getting more expensive every year. Nova Scotia spends more per capita than most provinces—$4,525 per person in 2005 compared with $4,438 for Canada overall. We have 39 hospitals, which is a lot for a province our size. Ontario has 13 times our population but only 6.6 times as many hospitals. According to the Canadian Medical Association, we had 219 physicians per 100,000 people, the highest among Canadian provinces and more than the overall Canadian figure of 200. The staff in the medical profession, I've found, is overwhelmingly courteous and professional. So it sounds like pretty good health care.

Of course there are concerns about wait times, as there are in every province in Canada (probably every jurisdiction in the world). Yet we're worse off on the East Coast than elsewhere. The Wait Time Alliance, which comprises thirteen medical bodies including the Canadian Medical Association, reported in June 2009 that Ontario, Manitoba, and British Columbia are strong performers in terms of wait times, while the Maritime provinces lag the rest of the country. To the government's credit, federal Health Minister Tony Clement has said Nova Scotia is a leader among the provinces in trying to reduce wait times. The government of Rodney MacDonald also deserves credit for trying to implement legislation that would prevent health care workers from going on strike or being locked out. The measure—which would have mimicked laws now in place in eight other provinces—would have ensured there is no interruption in health services during labour disputes and would allow the government more freedom in restructuring the health care system. Yet the New Democrats and Liberals prevented it from coming into law, lending some credence to the claims that the NDP was too cozy with unions to govern effectively.

Alas, there is one glaring hole in the health coverage offered by the Maritime provinces: We have virtually no universal drug coverage. Canadians living in every province from Quebec to the West Coast know the government will pay for their drugs in most cases if they contract a horrible illness. Maritimers do not. Some poor and elderly people are covered, and a lot of employees have medical benefits that include drug coverage. But the self-employed and many other employees are left to the tender mercies (and fine print) of health insurers if they want drugs paid for. The political left in Canada loves to decry the horrors of a two-tier health system that might occur if private medicine is allowed in Canada. But Canada already has a two-tier system, comprising a lower tier for Maritimers and a higher tier for everyone else. Let's say hypothetically that two unskilled labourers, one in Winnipeg and the other in Lunenburg, contract cancer. The one in Winnipeg is given the drugs he needs and lives and the one in Lunenburg dies. That certainly sounds like a two-tier system to me.

That's not any exaggeration. Cancer Care Statistics released in April 2008 show that Nova Scotians are more likely to die of cancer than any other Canadians. Nova Scotia has a cancer death rate for males of 245 per 100,000, compared to 178 in British Columbia and 209 nationally. For females, the corresponding numbers are 169 for Nova Scotia and 147 nationally. Of course the drug coverage is only one factor, but it's no doubt a significant factor. It's utterly appalling that the Canadian constitution and equalization programs supposedly ensure equal access to health care across the country, but so many Maritimers have no guarantee of the proper drugs if they get sick. "Atlantic Canada has lower rates of assistance for prescription drug coverage for cancer patients than other Canadian provinces," said a November 2006 press release from the Canadian Cancer Society's Newfoundland and Labrador chapter. "There are currently 600,000 Atlantic Canadian residents who do not have any drug coverage at all." Six hundred thousand people is one-quarter of the region's population. "We believe that no Canadian should have to choose between taking a drug they need and paying for their other basic needs," then-Liberal leader Stephane Dion said during the 2008 federal campaign, as reported by the *Toronto Star*. "Unfortunately, this is too often the case today, especially in the Atlantic provinces."

If this is not distressing enough, Nova Scotia's health care system faces deterioration unless it undergoes a "total transformation." That was the conclusion of a $1 million report by the Vancouver consultancy Corpus Sanchez in January 2008. The report made more than one hundred recommendations on how to improve the system, including closing emergency rooms at some rural hospitals. The report said emergency staff is performing duties that could be carried out at health clinics or doctors' offices. But once the report was released, the government flatly said that no rural emergency rooms would be closed.

This brings us to one of the largest problems with health care in the Maritimes—the questionable priorities of the government. A province the size of Nova Scotia, say health care experts, does not need thirty-nine hospitals, and this surplus leads to an excessive bureaucratic burden. John Ross, the outspoken former head of the emergency department of Capital Health (and, I should disclose, my cousin) puts it very well: We should stop pretending that all these emergency rooms scattered throughout the province can offer a complete range of services twenty-four-seven in each community. They can't. The staff simply isn't available. Ross said it would be better to have twenty-four-hour clinics throughout the province staffed by, for example, trained nurses, and backed up by a phone service for consultations. There would be four or five centres of excellence throughout the province able to provide a full range of medical services. Ross added that there simply has to be more teamwork among health care providers to get over the culture of each department head worrying only about his or her turf.

Another problem with the Nova Scotia health department came to light in 2009, and it was picked up by the Auditor General—the guy whose job a few years ago was simply to be on the lookout for government waste. Auditor General Jacques R. Lapointe reported in July 2009 that the government's preparations for the H1N1 flu (a.k.a. swine flu) were bogged down by burdensome bureaucracy. The report said the government drastically underspent its own estimate of what was needed to prepare for a pandemic, and as a result it will have insufficient supplies if the pandemic becomes serious. What's more, in 2008 the health department hired an external consultant to examine what should be done to prepare for a pandemic. As of July 2009, the consultant still had not reported.

## The Environment

You would think that Maritimers would enjoy better health than other places because we have few of the stresses of big cities, and our environment overall is cleaner than other places. Though our drinking water seems clear and the air is fresh, we have a few huge environmental problems that will take a generation and hundreds of millions of dollars to correct. In no particular order, we have to find solutions for our filthy electricity generation, the Sydney Tar Ponds, and our coastal sewage disposal. All of these solutions will require money, so once again our vulnerable economic position is restricting our ability to protect or improve our quality of life.

For generations, Nova Scotia was blessed with some of the world's richest coalfields. It's well known that the province once made the finest wooden ships in the world, but it's a lesser-known fact that in 1896 Nova Scotia was the world's sixth-largest producer of coal, a commodity as important at the time as oil is today. It always made sense for Nova

Scotia to generate electricity with our abundant coal, so most of our electricity plants are coal-fired. That has made Nova Scotia one of the worst producers of greenhouse gases from electricity production in the country. According to CIBC World Markets, Nova Scotia relied on coal, the dirtiest source of energy, for 60 percent of its energy in 2004, the third-worst level in Canada. In fact, the Maritimes comprise a little knot of dirty power within Canada. All the power generation on P.E.I. comes from oil, the second-dirtiest form of energy, while oil accounts for 40 percent of the generation in New Brunswick and 30 percent in Nova Scotia. In short, P.E.I., Nova Scotia, and New Brunswick are respectively the first, fourth, and fifth per capita producers of greenhouse gases in Canada, and numbers two and three are Alberta and Saskatchewan, whose booming economies make them better able to handle shocks in the energy markets.

This is particularly distressing because the world is moving to a system of carbon-trading mechanisms to encourage industry and consumers to use cleaner (or less) energy. Basically, every industry or jurisdiction would be given an allotment for carbon emissions, and would be taxed if it exceeded the allotment. If you produce less carbon dioxide than your allotment, you can sell what you don't need to another party that has exceeded its target. The details—such as whether the trading system would encompass a region, Canada, or all North America— still have to be worked out. But it is all but certain that such a system is coming, and Nova Scotia would exceed its allotment in a serious way.

"There are only a few jurisdictions in Canada, really Saskatchewan and Alberta, that are as exposed on carbon emissions as you are," said Tom Adams, the executive director of the Toronto-based consultancy Energy Probe. "And the more fragile economic circumstances [in the Maritimes] creates a certain vulnerability." Because of the Maritimes' high use of fossil fuels, if emission caps are introduced, then power rates would likely shoot up. So how much higher would they go in a place like Halifax, where consumers pay a basic rate and then 10.67 cents per kilowatt hour? "An extra cent per kilowatt hour is conceivable," Adams said, "and it could rise from there."

There is a chance for the Maritimes to prepare for this cap-and-trade system, but it will take some extraordinary diplomacy. In early 2009, the federal government struck a committee with the Atlantic provinces to be chaired by the Atlantic Canada Opportunities Agency to devise what they were calling the Atlantic Energy Gateway. No one has yet defined what this actually is; the federal government has only said it's designed to encourage the development of green energy and electricity exports to the U.S. Two things make this committee utterly intriguing, even though it has so far gained little media attention. First, it is absolutely critical to the development of all four Atlantic provinces, and second, the various provinces have greatly different interests. I suppose Nova Scotia and Prince Edward Island have similar goals—they both want a unified Atlantic Canadian power grid, so they can buy hydro power from Newfoundland and Labrador and find a market for their scattered green power projects. Newfoundland, meanwhile, wants to be able to export electricity from its 2,800-megawatt Lower Churchill power project to the lucrative New England market. Luciano Lisi, the founder of the green power producer Cape Breton Explorations Ltd., has argued that these goals can all be met by forming an Atlantic Energy Pool, which would be modeled on the ten-year-old New England Energy Pool. Under this proposal, the four Atlantic provinces would merge their grids, service the domestic market, and export the surplus to New England. It would include a cable under the Gulf of St. Lawrence to carry Lower Churchill power to Nova Scotia, then on to New

Brunswick and Maine. The pool would also provide a ready market for Lisi's projects in Cape Breton, wind farms around the region, tidal power in the Bay of Fundy, and the like. What's not to like about it?

Premier Shawn Graham has found one thing not to like. He believes New Brunswick would be better served by working with Hydro-Quebec, which he describes as the lowest-cost power producer in the world. He's struck two key alliances already—one with Hydro-Quebec and another with Maine governor John Baldacci. Graham is obviously hoping the Lower Churchill power will flow through Quebec, then New Brunswick, and on to New England. He told me in an interview that Nova Scotia could join in such a project, but geography is not in our favour. The dynamics here are fascinating, because conventional wisdom says Newfoundland and Labrador would prefer to avoid Quebec. Newfoundland and Labrador believes it got a raw deal in the 1960s agreement dividing the profits of the original Churchill Falls power, so it will be interesting to see if they do business with Quebec again.

We have no idea how this will work out, but Nova Scotia and P.E.I. will be greatly disadvantaged if they cannot access the enlarged grid. Nova Scotians' electricity rates, according to Adams, could rise 10 percent or more unless we find a credible means to use more green power. The trend of erecting wind farms won't do it because of the unreliability of wind. Experts believe Bay of Fundy tidal power, for all its wonders, will only produce about six hundred megawatts of power. As a result, Nova Scotia Power may have difficulty meeting its goal of having one-quarter of the province's electricity produced by renewable sources by 2015.

Nova Scotia's most famous environmental problem is the Sydney Tar Ponds—the toxic bog left by a century of steelmaking in the industrial centre. The contamination in four sites near the old steel mill has been called one of the worst environmental hotspots in Canada, but it still took about two decades of wrangling between the provincial and federal governments and the local community to come up with a plan to clean up the mess. In 2004, Ottawa and Nova Scotia signed a $400-million agreement on financing the job, but it took another three years to agree on a process. The plan calls for a process of solidification and stabilization—first by using a concrete to solidify the toxic bogs, and then applying a cocktail of chemicals to remove their harmful effects. However, the jury is out on whether this is the best means of cleaning the sites up. "It's a joke," said federal Green party leader Elizabeth May, who spent her formative years in Cape Breton. "It won't work. It's technically deeply flawed." May has said she would prefer a process that involves washing the soil to remove toxins, even though the agency responsible for the cleanup says such a method is unfeasible.

This cleanup plan has taken so long and is of such questionable worth in part because the province simply can't afford to conduct the cleanup on its own. If our economy were stronger, the provincial government could do it itself, or not have to spend so long bargaining so hard with Ottawa. But major environmental projects are delayed by decades of intergovernmental wrangling, which means the harm to the environment is exacerbated. Just as the Tar Ponds epic has been allowed to drag on for years, the federal, provincial, and municipal governments spent a generation haggling about sewage treatment plants for Halifax Harbour. The plants were first proposed in 1988, and construction began in 2005. By 2008, mayor Peter Kelly decreed that the new plants were having the desired effect and people would notice fewer "floatables" in Halifax harbour. The good mayor spoke too soon. In January 2009, a fifty-four-million-dollar plant near the Halifax waterfront broke down after a power outage, and has yet to be fixed. In the six months after that, more than eighty million litres of raw sewage flowed into Halifax Harbour every day, and it was expected to take another year to fix. The HRM council was refusing to release information about what exactly went wrong.

Even if the overall sewage treatment system worked, it may have been insufficient. When the governments built the $330-million facility, they only agreed on a primary waste disposal system. In April 2008, then-federal environment minister John Baird said Ottawa wanted communities across the country to install primary and secondary waste disposal systems to prevent sewage from entering waterways. Ottawa was prepared to put up $8 billion for the systems, but the total cost was estimated at $24 billion, requiring Canada's provinces and municipalities to pitch in $8 billion each. Halifax estimates it will cost a further $100 million to upgrade its system, but the capital city has it easier than most municipalities in the province. Most are starting from square one and will have to install primary and secondary systems all at once.

## Infrastructure and the Arts

These upgrades could prove difficult given that Nova Scotia already has the oldest infrastructure in the country and is estimated to need about $12.4 billion in investment to eradicate the so-called "infrastructure deficit." According to Statistics Canada, in February 2008 the average age of roads, bridges, overpasses, and sewer systems in Nova Scotia was 18 years in 2007, 1.7 years above the Canadian average. The average age of a Nova Scotia bridge or overpass was 28.6 years as of 2007, up from 24.2 years in 2001. In early 2009 the Conservative government tried to tap into federal stimulus funds to draw more money into the province to fix the infrastructure. But the money was slow in getting out of Ottawa, and then an election was called, and as of mid-2009 the new finance minister is working on his budget. It's difficult to say how our infrastructure deficit will be addressed.

Jurisdictions need sound infrastructure to generate economic growth, and there is another facet of the Maritime lifestyle that is essential for our economic prosperity—our culture. The fact is we need a strong cultural community much more than we need a fishery or manufacturing sector to increase the wealth of the province, and the economic impact of culture is now being studied as never before. Local artists have been talking about it for eons, though nobody listened. Alexa McDonough, when she led the Nova Scotia NDP in the 1980s, often spoke of the economic importance of culture, and again no one listened. Then Richard Florida burst on the scene. Florida, a professor and economic theorist, published a landmark study in 2002 called *The Rise of the Creative Class*, which stated that culture was an essential ingredient in economic development. It was a notion that had already gained currency in Europe, but the fact an American economist was propounding the theory made people sit up and take notice. Florida is respected enough that ACOA, Nova Scotia Business Inc., and the Greater Halifax Partnership flew him in to deliver a luncheon speech in Halifax in 2004. He told the enraptured audience that the modern knowledge-based economy relies on a strong, educated workforce, and such people tend to assemble in cities that have strong arts communities (bohemian and high-brow), a tolerant population, and a spirit that encourages creativity. On top of this, culture itself is a growth industry. Statistics Canada has reported that between 1971 and 2001, the Canadian culture sector labour force grew 160 percent, almost double the 81 percent growth in the labour force. Even the Conference Board of Canada has embraced the creative economy, saying it "extends beyond the culture sector to harness creativity in order to bring social and economic changes across a broad spectrum of industries, sectors and social organizations." Thus, there are two important components in cultural policy: first, it adds immeasurable vibrancy to a community and defines its inhabitants; second, it is key to modern economic growth. So how does Nova Scotia—and by implication the Maritimes—fare in the cultural economy?

Good and bad.

Looking at things objectively, anyone can see there are some remarkable artistic successes in Nova Scotia—the musical *Drum!*, novels like Alistair MacLeod's *No Great Mischief*, and Ami McKay's *The Birth House*, the TV show and movie "The Trailer Park Boys," and the blossoming East Coast music scene. The Nova Scotia College of Art and Design is an absolute gem whose graduates have made an astonishing contribution to our cultural industries. (NSCAD president David Smith likes to note that 75 percent of his graduates follow entrepreneurial pursuits after graduation.) What's more, Halifax scores very well in assessments of creative communities. We have a lot to be proud of.

The bad news is that Nova Scotian artists are struggling to produce these works amid a climate of neglect (some say contempt) from the provincial government. There is an innately creative community in the province and it's struggling with a lack of investment and funding. Cultural communities around the world need government and corporate support, and if that support is available the economic returns can be magnificent. But Nova Scotia is failing to capitalize on this resource.

The numbers match what we've seen in other facets of life in Nova Scotia. According to StatsCan numbers compiled by Andrew Terris, a principal with the advocacy group Arts Nova, Nova Scotia ranks seventh in Canada in arts funding per capita. For the 2004–2005 fiscal year, we placed eighth in provincial funding in each of the three core cultural segments—literary arts, performing arts, and visual arts and crafts. "The core creative fields in Nova Scotia have been on a starvation diet for 30 years," said Terris. What's more, culture is declining as a priority for the Nova Scotia government. Between 2000 and 2008, overall government expenses rose 48.7 percent, but arts and culture funding rose 21.8 percent. One other problem with cultural funding is much of it is consumed by the Nova Scotia Tattoo, which is essentially a tourist attraction and does little to develop the artistic community. In 2009, the federal government said it would kick in $460,000 to promote the production overseas and $500,000 for a new sound system and marketing. That money would be better used in developing bona fide artistic endeavors, where Nova Scotia is grossly underfunded. The only segments in which the province does well is arts education (second), multiculturalism (fourth), and heritage (fifth). The saving grace for arts in Nova Scotia is that we rank third per capita in federal arts funding, which has benefited mainly film, television, and broadcasting.

Arts administrators constantly say that we need a greater investment in infrastructure. Some mean physical structures—theatres, repertory cinema, sound stages, editing rooms, auditoriums, and art galleries. But beyond this, we are lacking the funding in the administrative organizations that support artists. We need to develop these institutions that develop and market art.

As a rule I am skeptical about the role of cultural administrators, but I've seen the remarkable job done by the Writers' Federation of Nova Scotia on a shoestring budget. With only two full-time staffers, it works with publishers to help distribute and promote books, publishes weekly and quarterly newsletters, organizes the annual book festival and the Word on the Street exhibition, and oversees mentorship programs, contests, and writers' visits to schools and seminars. The federation is instrumental in engendering an environment in which literature can endure—not thrive, but endure. It does all this on a grant of $68,000 from the province (roughly one-third of the expenses of an average MLA). The Nova Scotia government also contributes about $150,000 annually to book publishers. That compares with about $4.6 million in grants and tax credits for publishers from the Ontario government. Yes, Ontario is a big province, so the comparison is unfair. But look at Manitoba, with only slightly more people than Nova Scotia. It grants book publishers $262,000 annually, magazine publishers $206,000, and the publishers association $49,000. On top of that, it makes $114,000 in annual payments to the writers' guild and $210,000 in grants to writers and other artists.

The fact our artists receive less support than their confreres in other provinces is only part of the story. The artistic community—and remember, we're talking about the captains of a growth industry—still feel utterly betrayed by the closing of the Nova Scotia Arts Council in 2002. As government decisions go, it was comparable to prime minister Stephen Harper's claim that he cut arts funding because it goes to champagne receptions. Both were stupid, economically damaging, and politically foolish. In the Nova Scotia case, the arts council had been an arms-length organization of artists and administrators that worked with the government to develop the arts. Artsy types admit the council had its problems and suffered from too much infighting from the various sectors, but closing the organization was dastardly, they say. The government of John Hamm unilaterally closed it down the day before Good Friday, sequestering the staff to explain what was happening, ushering them out of the building, and padlocking the office. The council was replaced with Nova Scotia Arts and Culture Partnership Council, whose board is made up largely of arts representatives but is generally viewed by the cultural community as more an extension of the government than the arts council was.

What the arts community wants is a restoration of the arts council, and I would support such a move. In fact, I think we should go beyond that and try to work with New Brunswick and Prince Edward Island to create a Maritimes Arts Council. Or add in Newfoundland and Labrador for an Atlantic Canadian council. The larger council would have three advantages. First, it could probably distribute more money to Maritime artists than three separate groups. As well as achieving economies of scale, the regional body could argue strongly that it is promoting a growth industry across the three provinces and therefore seek ACOA funding. It would be larger than the sum of its parts. Second, the regional body could do more for the region's physical infrastructure. Maybe Halifax needs sound stages while New Brunswick needs more libraries. I don't know the particulars, but a larger body would be more efficient in developing infrastructure than a patchwork of little groups. Finally, the regional group could undertake marketing more easily, expanding the arts community's domestic market and increasing profit.

## Public Safety

The final lifestyle element we should consider is public safety and crime, especially in the Halifax area, where this has become an important issue. In 2006 StatsCan conducted a survey of twenty-four thousand people across Canada to find out if they had been victims of such crimes as robbery, sexual or physical assault, or breaking and entering in a twelve-month period. The Halifax metropolitan area had the highest rate of violent incidents per capita in the country. The statistics agency said there were seventy-one thousand violent incidents in 2004, for a rate of 229. Toronto had more incidents, but its rate was 107. Though the crime rate improved in the ensuing two years, Halifax has witnessed some horrific crimes in the recent past—the stabbing of an American sailor in a downtown bar, a Dartmouth teen tortured for hours by two teenage girls, a double knife murder in Glen Haven.

"This isn't a figment of someone's imagination," Dalhousie University criminologist Don Clairmont told the municipal council in May 2008 after releasing a 650-page, sixty-eight-thousand-dollar study into crime in the city. He said the overwhelming evidence shows there is a "serious problem of violence and public safety in HRM." He recommended developing a full-time public safety co-ordinator, improving race relations, and broadening the responsibilities of Halifax's police forces as the first steps in curbing violent crime. Mayor Peter Kelly responded by saying his council would consider the report, but there are no funds in place to implement its recommendations—a poor excuse for a council that had helped blow $9.5 million on a failed bid for the Commonwealth Games and seems obsessed with finding ways for rock stars to play concerts on the Commons.

## What's Needed

It's easy to conclude that there are downsides to life in the Maritimes. Much as it's a lovely place to live, we are at the lower end of public service performance in Canada. In all of these categories—education, health, environment, infrastructure, culture, crime prevention—we have to aim for Canadian averages. There is no reason why Maritimers can't access the same level of service from their government or publicly funded bodies as the residents of other provinces. Let's be frank: getting the services we deserve is not going to come without tough action somewhere. We would have to cut university tuitions by one-fifth to meet the national average, and that should be the target within five years. As other universities are raising their tuition fees, we should be cutting ours so that we're in the middle of the pack. Students who attend university here don't get a better education than students in other provinces, so there's no reason they should emerge from university with more debt than their peers to the west (or northeast for that matter). Reducing tuition should be a key initiative to keeping young people in the Maritimes—let's first reduce their need to pay down debt, then more of them may be able to afford to stay here. The best way to cut costs would be to merge the Halifax universities, reducing and centralizing all administrative offices. (The one possible exception might be the Nova Scotia College of Art and Design, because it's such a specialist institution and so superb at what it does.) The result would be a single institution with about twenty-eight thousand full- and part-time students, just over one-third the size of the seventy-five-thousand-student body at University of Toronto. It would be a shame to lose the heritage of the distinct universities, the SMU–Dal rivalry, and the neighbourhood feeling that comes with small institutions. But we would gain a larger university of higher standing, one with greater centres of excellence for research, and our students could be educated at less expense. Nova Scotia should "create a University of Nova Scotia or, minimally, an HRM-based University of Halifax, and concentrate excellence through program consolidation on campuses with demonstrated strengths," said academics Anthony Davis and Michael Whalen in a July 2009 opinion piece in the *Chronicle Herald*. They added that universities should consolidate such administrative services as "admissions, recruitment, finance, library, procurement, and presidential/vice-presidential offices to create efficiencies and savings." If the Halifax and/or Nova Scotia universities did consolidate wholly or in part to save money, other Maritime universities would have to respond to the lower costs.

In health care, Nova Scotia needs to have the debate that it has long avoided: do we want to continue financing rural hospitals and emergency rooms or centralize health care? Again, I believe we should aim for the national average, which would mean reducing the number of hospitals in the province and consolidating some rural facilities. This is an incredibly hot topic outside the Halifax area, and understandably so. I live in the country and have had to drive forty-five minutes to reach a hospital—I know it's inconvenient at the best of times and worrying in an emergency. But we should be aiming for a system that provides drug coverage for everyone, and to do that we may have to reduce the number of hospitals and emergency wards. We also have to accept that people in the modern world should be given the option of buying private health insurance.

To recap: the Maritimes are facing a demographic crisis, and young people are moving out of the province, so we need to build an economic environment that will draw people here. But we offer lower pay than elsewhere in Canada and generally poorer social services. As I've said throughout, we should look at a policy of moderation and consolidation. We should be working with the other Maritime provinces to build larger and more cost-efficient institutions, and raise our public service performance measure out of the Canadian basement.

# *public finances*

## chapter five

*T*he distance from Halifax City Hall to the World Trade and Convention Centre is about thirty metres. But on April 17, 2008, they might as well have been in different universes.

At the trade centre that night, the great and the good of Halifax turned out for the Halifax Chamber of Commerce's annual dinner, which featured a speech by the most revered living Maritime politician, Frank McKenna. McKenna had spent the decade to 1997 as premier of New Brunswick, then became the Canadian ambassador to Washington in 2005. He's now the vice-chairman of TD Bank, the best-managed Canadian bank. No one in public life in the region can match his resumé, and he used the weight of his celebrity to deliver a simple message to Nova Scotians and other Maritimers: cut taxes. "Number one is taxes," McKenna said in his speech, as reported in the *Chronicle Herald*. "The world is changing under our feet in terms of taxes. We have got to get lower personal and corporate taxes in this region."

McKenna called for Nova Scotia and New Brunswick to reform their taxes. The federal government had recently knocked two percentage points off its harmonized sales tax, and the former New Brunswick premier advocated adding those two percentage points to the consumption tax and using additional revenues to cut corporate and personal income taxes. He noted the rest of the world is cutting income taxes, and that even leftist administrations in Eastern Europe are slashing rates by as much as twenty percentage points. This is the global economy that the Maritime provinces must compete in. "It's a world that in some ways is passing us by," said McKenna.

But this plea for a more efficient tax system contrasted sharply with what had happened across the street a few hours earlier. The Halifax Regional Council was wrapping up its budget deliberations and looking at another property tax increase. Krista Snow, the councillor for Waverley–Fall River–Beaver Bank, surprised her colleagues by asking that the council send the budget back to staff to cut expenditures and hold the line on taxes. Other councillors said such a request should have been made two months earlier. Reg Rankin, the councillor for Timberlea–Prospect, said it would "border on abuse" to ask the municipality's staff to go back and look for savings.

In the end council decided to increase tax rates by 2.6 percent. Given that property assessments rose an average of 3.1 percent for the year, it meant that property taxes in Nova Scotia's largest municipality rose 5.7 percent for the year. That's almost twice the rate of inflation. Given that my family's property taxes have doubled since we moved into our house six years ago, I was angered by it. No doubt, I wasn't alone.

Now, McKenna was talking about income taxes and the council set property taxes. But the juxtaposition of these two episodes manifests a huge problem we have in Nova Scotia—we're overtaxed. The governments that tax us so highly don't seem to appreciate that it's bad policy, bad economics, and probably bad politics. We're taxed more than other Canadians on what we earn, what we spend, the houses we buy, the houses we build, the car we drive, the gas we put into that car, the beer we drink, the cigarettes we smoke, the assets we sell. (If a carbon tax comes in, they'll tax the air we breathe. You knew it would happen eventually.) In every enterprise Nova Scotians undertake throughout our lives, the government takes a bigger slice than if we had done it somewhere west of the Tantramar Marsh.

## New Brunswick's Reforms

Because while Frank McKenna may have been ignored at Halifax City Hall and down the hill at Province House, his successor in New Brunswick was listening. In March 2009, New Brunswick premier Shawn Graham and his finance minister, Victor Boudreau, stunned their province by bringing in a budget that would cut taxes and reduce the size of government. After a year-long review of its tax system, New Brunswick was shaving about $144 million off its personal income tax receipts in 2009–2010, and that number would increase to $323 million by 2012. But that was just the reduction in personal income taxes. The budget also reduced the corporate tax rate to 12 percent from 13 percent in the first year, and outlined a plan to cut the corporate income tax rate to 8 percent within three years. The news was not all good. New Brunswick cut 700 government positions (including the positive move of not filling 300 vacant positions) and the province was forecasting a $265 million deficit in the first year. The budget received little notice outside New Brunswick, largely because Canadians were focused on the larger international recession, but think tanks and business groups sat up and took notice. "Thank God for New Brunswick," said Leanne Hachey of the Canadian Federation of Small Business during a discussion on the outlook of the Maritime economy. Sadly for Graham, the ratings agency took notice as well. In August 2009, Moody's Investors Service Ltd. cut New Brunswick's debt rating one notch to Aa2 because of the "sizeable" increase in borrowing forecast over four years. This lends some legitimacy to the Nova Scotia government's claim that it has to proceed with more caution than New Brunswick has. "The tax proposal in New Brunswick will add to their debt by $2.2 billion over the next couple of years," said premier Darrell Dexter in an interview. "We're just not in a position to add to our debt in that fashion."

There's no question that Graham was pursuing a policy he felt was best for New Brunswick, but it's also clear that he had one eye on Nova Scotia when he conceived his tax cuts. He understands the two provinces are competing for talent, capital, and businesses, and the tax cuts will give New Brunswick a huge advantage. Based on current projections, Nova Scotia is due to maintain its corporate tax rate at 16 percent—tied with P.E.I. for the highest in Canada—while the New Brunswick rate is falling. "New Brunswick, once fully implemented by 2012, will have a corporate tax rate of 8 percent, half of the province of Nova Scotia, which will put us in the driver's seat for economic development here in Atlantic Canada and across the country," Graham said in a speech in Moncton three months after introducing his budget.

New Brunswick, in fact, got a jump on Nova Scotia partly because of a tragedy. Michael Baker, Nova Scotia's finance minister in Rodney MacDonald's government, had begun a tax review at the same time as New Brunswick. Business leaders were hoping the two provinces would work together on the review, and the provinces said they would consult, but it was never more than lip service. I interviewed both Baker and Boudreau during their reviews, and it seemed obvious that the New Brunswick government was more determined to fundamentally alter the way it taxed its citizens. Sadly, Baker died of cancer early in 2009 without having completed his tax review. The study was set aside while the finance department prepared the 2009–2010 budget, then the government changed, and as of the summer of 2009 the review seems to be on hold as new finance minister Graham Steele prepares his own budget for Nova Scotia.

When Steele, a smart and personable lawyer, presented his budget in September 2009, the province had a $592 million deficit, a drop from an official surplus of $20 million a year earlier. Program expenditures rose 6.7 percent to $9.1 billion, and most worrying, the provincial debt rose to an historic high of $13.5 billion. (The debt had previously crested three years earlier at $12.4 billion, then edged lower. Now it was growing again.) It's the type of budget that would normally have me hollering at the TV set in disgust during the evening news. But I think the media have been correct in cutting Steele some slack with his debut budget. He has inherited a dire financial position during an economic crisis, and he was adjusting from opposition to government. I could even see critics accepting a mild improvement in 2010–2011. But Steele has to bring in significant reforms by his third budget, because Nova Scotia in the age of globalization cannot perpetuate a big government–high tax–high debt model. He and Dexter have to reduce spending and lower taxes.

## Corporate Taxes

Let's start with the corporate taxes that Shawn Graham touched on in his Moncton speech. Simply put, businesses in Nova Scotia and P.E.I. are taxed more than companies elsewhere. The federal government imposes a 19 percent income tax on corporations across the country, which is due to decline to 18 percent in 2010, and each province then imposes its own corporate tax on top of that. These provincial rates range from 10 percent in Alberta to 16 percent in Nova Scotia and P.E.I. That total rate of 35 percent in these two provinces is the highest in Canada (though not North America—California has a corporate tax rate of 43.8 percent). Small businesses in Nova Scotia pay a total tax rate of 18.12 percent, which puts the province in a three-way tie for the third-highest tax on small enterprises in Canada. (Nova Scotia classifies small businesses as those with less than four hundred thousand dollars in annual revenues, while New Brunswick has just raised its threshold to five hundred thousand dollars.)

This business income tax is not a big deal in terms of generating income for the province, because it raises only about $320 million to $420 million a year—roughly enough to finance the province's operations for two or three weeks. But it is has a lot of economic importance. First of all, a high corporate tax rate deters companies from setting up offices in Halifax. It's not the only factor, but if a company is considering where to establish an office that generates profits, corporate taxes will be one factor it examines. What is even worse about the high corporate tax rate is the effect it has on businesses that are already here. A high tax rate eats into a company's bottom line, leaving lower retained earnings to reinvest in equipment and technology. Chapter three discussed how the problem of low productivity in the region was caused by a lack of investment in plant and equipment, and high corporate taxes contribute to that problem.

There's another problem with high corporate taxes: they're contributing to Nova Scotia's estrangement from the rest of Canada. In October 2007 federal finance minister Jim Flaherty announced that his government wanted Canada to have the lowest corporate taxes in the Group of Seven industrialized countries. Whether he succeeds is open to debate, because developed and developing countries around the world are lowering corporate tax rates. But he has already begun the downward movement. In 2008, the federal rate dropped from 22.12 percent to 19.5 percent, and it's due to be trimmed to 15 percent by 2013. That program is estimated to cut more than $14 billion from the taxes businesses pay. But Ottawa only controls a portion of the corporate income tax, and Flaherty called on the provinces to drop their corporate taxes as well so the country could have a broad-based plan to lower the burden on businesses. That call led to a very public spat with Ontario premier Dalton McGuinty, who disagreed with Flaherty's assertion that Ontario's corporate tax was too high. The fact is that Nova Scotia's corporate rate is two to four percentage points higher than Ontario's, but the finance minister didn't bother to pick a fight on that count. Nova Scotia made no response on what it plans to do about its corporate rate, likely because the finance department is leery of doing anything that would cut revenue. My own feeling is the downside in cutting the corporate income tax is limited because even in a good year the tax accounts for only about $420 million in revenue. Meanwhile in New Brunswick, Shawn Graham began to note in interviews that the country's corporate rates were falling, and New Brunswick would be participating in the goal of imposing the most competitive corporate taxes in the developed world. The Nova Scotia government had an opportunity to join an initiative sponsored by the federal treasury and boost its economy in the process. But so far, the government has been silent on the matter.

## Personal Taxes

It's more difficult to compare the personal income tax rate among the provinces, because personal taxes are progressive—meaning the more money you make, the higher your tax rate is. The federal and provincial governments have different levels at which the higher tax rates kick in.

But here are some things to note about the Nova Scotia government's component of the income tax: Nova Scotia applies an 8.79 percent rate on its lowest tax band, which is in the middle of the pack among Canadian provinces. That means the poorest people in Nova Scotia—as they should—pay nearly the same income tax as people of similar income across the country. But Nova Scotians move out of that first tax band when their income hits $29,590, the lowest level in Canada, and once income rises above that threshold, the tax rate rises aggressively. The two middle bands have a tax rate of 14.95 percent and 16.67 percent, which is higher than the 9–13 percent range common in central and western provinces. The top rate in Nova Scotia is 17.5 percent, the second highest rate after Quebec.

What this means to John and Jane Q. Public is that they have less spending power than they would in other provinces. We've seen already that people can earn less money in Nova Scotia and still pay a higher tax rate than in other provinces. But take a look at how the taxes cut into a family's income. Let's say a one-income family has an income of $52,700—the average in Canada according to StatsCan. In Ontario, that family will pay taxes of $10,682, in Manitoba $12,781, in British Columbia $10,325, and in Nova Scotia $12,878.

Finally there is the HST, created in 1997 to harmonize the federal goods and services tax and the provincial sales tax. Nova Scotia, New Brunswick, and Newfoundland and Labrador all implemented the tax in a rare bout of interprovincial harmony, and it now stands at 13 percent, which is a higher rate than the combined GST and provincial sales tax in the central and western provinces. What's good about the HST is that it applies to three provinces and suggests the Maritimes (and the Atlantic provinces) can harmonize some aspects of their economies. But what is most insidious about the tax is that it covers a range of services as well as goods. Before the GST came along in 1989, the visible sales tax was only the provincial tax and it only applied to goods. Brian Mulroney's 7 percent tax applied to both goods and services. So in the pre-HST days, if you wanted to hire a decorator in Nova Scotia, for example, you only had to pay the 7 percent GST. The creation of the HST lowered the overall rate somewhat, but it extended the provincial sales tax to services as well as goods. The result is that the provinces covered by the HST generally raise more sales tax than other provinces, not only because the rate is high but also because the tax applies to so many things. For example, in the last chapter I mentioned Mark Whalen, who moved to Nova Scotia from Alberta. He bought an all-terrain vehicle before he left Alberta, but didn't register it until he got to Nova Scotia. In Alberta, there is no tax at all on registering an ATV but in Nova Scotia there was the 14 percent (at that time) HST. Mark was slapped with the tax.

One area where the HST is particularly harsh is when it's applied to new home construction. This is a matter that is now being hotly debated in Ontario and British Columbia as those provinces consider adopting the HST. BMO Financial noted in a report on the HST that home construction is one segment of the economy that could be jeopardized under the plan. In fact, it said housing starts fell 23 percent in Atlantic Canada when the three eastern provinces harmonized their sales tax. The provincial and federal governments both offer rebates on the sales tax applied to new homes, but Nova Scotians buying a new home have been hit far harder than people elsewhere. Of course, Nova Scotia will be on the same footing as other provinces if the HST becomes the norm across the country.

We have another high sales tax in Nova Scotia that might be a good thing: the excise tax on gasoline. I say it might be good because there are a number of ways of evaluating it. Any tax is going to drain money from the economy and make it less efficient. Certainly, Shawn Graham helped his economy when he lowered New Brunswick's fuel tax 3.8 cents a litre when he took office in October 2006. (And it's just as certain that he hurt the economy when he raised other taxes in his first budget.) At the other end of the country, British Columbia was taking another approach. Early in 2008, B.C. said it would phase in a comprehensive carbon tax in an attempt to encourage a reduction in greenhouse gases. The part of this tax to be imposed on gasoline resulted in an increase of 2.41 cents per litre as of July 1, 2008, rising to 7.24 cents a litre by 2012. This tax will probably not damage the B.C. economy because it was balanced with cuts in other taxes and direct payments to consumers, and it appears extremely enlightened given the current environmental and geopolitical climate. Liberals around the world are advocating such taxes, not just for ecological reasons. Since the terrorist attacks of September 11, 2001, *New York Times* columnist Thomas Friedman has been obsessed with the thought of the U.S. imposing carbon taxes to encourage new energy technologies, wean America off foreign oil, and reduce the income of Middle Eastern states that are financing terrorism.

Nova Scotia does not have a carbon tax per se, but it might as well have one. Even when the B.C. carbon tax came into effect in 2008, the total taxation on a litre of gas in Nova Scotia exceeded that of B.C. The precise tax rate varies depending on the price of gas, but if the price is at 1 dollar per litre in Nova Scotia, the federal and provincial tax component in that price is 39.4 cents. That is exceeded only by 40.5 cents in Newfoundland and Labrador. The British Columbia tax, after the first phase of the carbon tax is introduced, would be about 33.3 cents. So we are in theory doing our bit ecologically by putting up with a high tax on gasoline, but the economic effects are harsh.

One more major tax we should consider is the property taxes imposed by the municipalities. As we previously saw, a homeowner pays a tax rate of 0.8548 percent of the assessed value of a home in Toronto, 0.50 percent in Calgary, and 1.347 percent in Halifax—60 percent more than Toronto. But that's not the worst of it. The biggest problem is how quickly property assessments and taxes have risen in HRM. I can use my own home as an example. I bought it in 2003 and the municipal property taxes were $2,400. I've made no renovations other than building a tree house in the backyard (and it's not that great a tree house), yet five years later I find myself paying taxes of about $5,100. I think the more than doubling of property tax in five years is extreme even for the Halifax area, but it can happen.

One problem with high property taxes is they are especially cruel to pensioners. It's not uncommon for people to receive less in retirement than they were hoping for, and pensioners are known to pinch the odd penny, largely because they have to. I've never met a pensioner who budgeted for their property taxes to double in five or six years, but a lot of them face that prospect. They're powerless to stop it, and many of them for health reasons can't go back to the workforce to raise their income. They haven't moved anywhere, so it's not like they've been extravagant. They just have increasing amounts of their fixed income nibbled away by rising property taxes.

There's something unsettling about the way the Nova Scotia government collects its taxes, because the provincial tax system hurts the people least able to pay. I mentioned that Nova Scotia's tax rate for the absolute poorest people is the same as most other provinces, as it should be. But by imposing a higher rate for the HST than the combined sales tax of other provinces, the provincial government is reducing the spending power of the people least able to pay. The same goes for high gasoline taxes.

Economists generally advise that consumption taxes (like the HST) are preferable to income taxes because a low income tax encourages investment and improves productivity. So most economists consider the Harper government's two-percentage point cut in the GST a waste of money because it did little to improve productivity, whereas a cut in income tax would have helped a lot. What befuddled me during the debate about the HST/GST cuts was the Centre for Policy Alternatives denouncing these consumption tax cuts, saying they favour the rich. Nothing could be further from the truth. Any family trying to get by on twenty-eight thousand dollars a year has to account for every penny, and it likely felt the drop in sales tax more than anyone. Sales taxes punish the poor far more than the rich, even though the rich spend more, and Nova Scotia is punishing its poor by maintaining such a high rate of HST.

Let's conclude with a sweeping statement: taxes in Nova Scotia and Prince Edward Island are among the highest in Canada, while New Brunswick is aggressively lowering its taxes. No one can argue with that. Taxes here are broad and high and the taxman's bony fingers reach into every cranny of life. The Nova Scotia government has ignored the problem for at least a generation. For as far back as I can remember, business organizations have been screaming for lower taxes, and the government has been deaf to their entreaties. The government could not easily lower taxes twenty years ago because of the horrendous deficits it was running up. After recording seven balanced budgets in a row, Nova Scotia is now in a purgatory of red ink again, and there is only one solution. With New Brunswick cutting taxes so aggressively, Nova Scotia has little room to raise revenues. Even once the books are balanced, Steele will have to cut spending to lower taxes.

One thing to note about the whole history of deficit financing in this period is it has sullied the legacy of both Savage (premier from 1993 to 1997) and the other dominant premier of the time—Progressive Conservative John Buchanan (1978–90). Buchanan, a master at grassroots glad-handing, is generally remembered as the premier who built up the province's debt. It's a reputation he deserves, as his was a profligate government. Yet it's a shame that this reputation overrides his good work on two fronts—creating a sense of business optimism that shielded Nova Scotia somewhat from the blight of the 1981 recession; and working successfully with the federal government and other provinces on constitutional and economic initiatives. The late Dr. Savage also deserves a better reputation than he has earned. He took over a dreadful fiscal situation and cleaned it up, and the shame of it is the last Tory government undid a lot of his good work. Though he came from the left of the political spectrum, he took measures that could only please the right by courageously curtailing public sector spending growth and addressing the problem of the growing deficit. Savage took the steps needed to reign in spending, and his unpopular actions allowed John Hamm to stabilize the situation early in the new century. However, it took years for the effects of a supposedly balanced budget to be felt on the overall net debt. Even after the budget was balanced the net direct debt kept growing. Even Darrell Dexter—supposedly running to the ideological left of the incumbent Tories—campaigned in the spring of 2009 on the baffling fact that Nova Scotia supposedly had seven years of balanced budget, but the debt kept growing.

Unfortunately, that debt is growing again. In 2006–2007, it crested at $12.4 billion then edged downwards slightly, and for the 2008–2009 fiscal year it was $12.3 billion. Then the stimulus package came along, and all of a sudden we're going from deep in debt to deeper in debt. What's troubling is that we seem to be reversing the discipline instilled in the 1990s. The most important measurement in assessing debt is the net direct debt as a proportion of GDP, and that measurement has been shrinking steadily due to the creeping economic growth. The measurement had fallen from 48.7 percent in 1999–2000 to an estimated 34.9 percent for 2008–2009. Now that level is rising again toward the 40 percent mark—among the worst in Canada. Finally, there's no way anyone can argue that Nova Scotia needed to grow our debt this large since New Brunswick has far less debt than Nova Scotia. Our provinces are largely subject to the same economic forces, yet New Brunswick's political leaders have been responsible enough to keep a tighter reign on their spending. Even though our next-door neighbour has increased its spending on highways recently, its net direct debt is only $7.1 billion, or 26 percent of GDP.

When he was campaigning to become premier, Darrell Dexter spoke eloquently about the need to lower Nova Scotia's debt, and it will be interesting to see how great a priority it becomes now that he's in power. It's depressing that the government of Rodney MacDonald attached such a low priority to curing debt woes. His government tossed a few million toward debt reduction each year, and the debt shrank by $12.3 million or 0.1 percent in 2008–2009. His predecessor, John Hamm, attached more importance to the mission of paying down debt. When Nova Scotia received an $830 million windfall from the federal-provincial offshore oil agreement, Hamm decreed that the entire amount would go toward debt reduction. In addition, in 2004 the legislature passed a bill requiring all "extraordinary revenue" be used to reduce the provincial debt. That legislation defined extraordinary revenue as income "not included in the annual budget." It remains law today. But in the winter of 2007–2008, the government found an extraordinary revenue of $300 million, and the money went to infrastructure projects rather than debt reduction.

Nova Scotia now pays $889 million a year to service its debt—the third-largest item on the budget. Although it's an improvement from $964 million three years ago, it's still a massive liability. If interest rates rise, those debt-servicing costs could be forced higher. Most important, as long as our debt is so massive, the government is severely restricted in its ability to cut taxes. Tax cuts will be monitored closely by the ratings agencies, and if they don't like what the province is doing then they could lower our credit ratings, which again would increase the amount we spend to service the debt. The debt is less of a problem than it was a decade ago, but it is still a huge blight on our finances. The first thing the government must do with our money is pay interest on debt, then all the other government operations are piled on top of those payments. This is less of a problem in most other provinces, because most have less debt as a percentage of GDP than we do.

So what is the overall effect of all these high taxes? No one likes to pay them, but there is something more than annoyance at play here. We can see it when we consider the overall effect of these and other taxes imposed by the provincial government. The problem is that so much of our output is devoted to what is essentially dead money. I can feel opponents squirming at the suggestion that taxation is dead money. At first glance, I can understand their chagrin. Surely money raised through taxes goes to supporting schools, hospitals, and all the services the government provides for us.

## Dead Money

We are coming to one of the kernels of this book's thesis. We've established in this chapter that Nova Scotia has some of the highest personal and corporate income taxes, sales taxes, and property taxes in the country. Just as you would want a Mercedes if you pay fifty thousand dollars for a car, you would expect that Nova Scotians would have the best services in the country if we pay the most taxes. At the very least, you'd expect the government services to be mid-level. But we have seen that statistically we have some of the poorest school results, highest death rates from cancer, highest university tuitions, highest crime rates, and oldest infrastructure in the country. We Nova Scotians pay the most and get the least. When I had a column in the *Chronicle Herald*, I would frequently denounce the tax structures in the province, and as often as not I'd get an email from some well-meaning but mistaken soul saying we need high taxes to pay for government programs. But there has to be some connection between the amount we pay and what we get in return. We are paying thirty bucks a plate to eat at McDonald's.

Tax levels do matter. It's amazing that this needs to be emphasized, but so much of the political debate in the Maritimes assumes that taxes will remain at current levels. The fact is we are harming our future economic performance with high taxes. People don't want to move to places with high taxes. Long-time residents become somewhat anesthetized by high taxes and learn to live with them, but for people moving here from other spots, taxes are like a smack across the face with a dead flounder. High taxes are a reason to leave (or not to come in the first place). Second, high taxes stifle economic growth.

Experts on both the right and left can point to practical examples of tax cuts respectively propelling and thwarting economic growth. Conservatives hail president John F. Kennedy's tax cuts of almost 2 percent of GDP in 1963–64 as adding almost a percentage point of GDP growth to the U.S. economy by the late 1960s. Similarly, they argue that president Ronald Reagan's tax cuts in 1980–81 fuelled the booms of the late 1980s. Liberals and social democrats can just as easily argue that president George W. Bush's tax cuts didn't give much of a lift to the economy late in his administration, and former Ontario premier Mike Harris's tax cuts saddled the province with massive deficits and left the province in its worst economic position ever within Confederation.

Who's right? I'd say the conservatives are. Both Bush and Harris cut taxes without placing corresponding restraints on government spending—a policy that's fine to ignite a flagging economy but simply does not work over the long haul. Even Ronald Reagan had to increase taxes later in his term, and his successor, the elder George Bush, famously raised taxes in 1990. That move probably cost him re-election in 1992, but it also set the stage for the profound economic growth of the Clinton years. Nova Scotia needs tax cuts because our taxes are out of whack with the rest of the country. We need more money in consumers' pockets, and we need businesses to retain more of their profits to reinvest in their business. That's essential to improving productivity, so that we can do more with fewer workers, and it's essential to generate economic growth ahead of a wave of workers leaving the workforce. But we have to make sure we don't run deficits or add to the debt.

Should we follow McKenna's advice and increase the HST to lower income taxes? My answer is no. A two-percentage-point hike in the HST would whack poor people disproportionately and is unfair, and in the current economic slowdown an increase in sales tax would hamper consumer spending power. What's more, the HST is still higher than most other consumption taxes in Canada, and as ever we want a policy of moderation. We should leave the HST where it is for now, but we should still aim for income taxes that are around the Canadian average.

Nova Scotia should lower the 16 percent business tax to about 14 percent, and continue to lower it in the coming years until we achieve parity with New Brunswick. The business tax brought in about $450 million in good times, so the government would have to cut about $200 million to $250 million in spending to pay for the tax cut. Personal income taxes are far more complicated, but we need to aim for a middle band rate of 13 percent and a top rate of 15 percent. To make the whole program politically viable, we should probably also lop a percentage point off the lowest band. Overall, Nova Scotia's personal income taxes would still be above the national average, but we'd be closer to the middle. In a back-of-the-envelope calculation, I would bet this would cost about $270 million, so these cuts in total would probably cost about $500 million. That sounds like a lot, but remember that Nova Scotia government revenue came in $300 million over budget in 2007–2008, so there can be multi-million-dollar upside surprises in revenue.

Of course, we'd want to effect those tax cuts without moving into a structural deficit. (We'll probably have a couple years of deficits because of the global recession, but we'll want balanced budgets once the world recovers.) Could $500 million be trimmed from the provincial budget? I believe it could and will show how in the coming chapters. Besides, if Nova Scotia reduces taxes by $500 million and makes its economy more efficient, economic growth would improve and some of that money would find its way back into government coffers.

# *public sector*

## chapter six

*H*ere's a question that strikes at the heart of economic studies: Is a large public sector good or bad for a jurisdiction's economy?

Most mainstream economists—and all conservative ones—will tell you that an excessively large public sector will, over time, constrain economic growth because governments spend money, while private enterprises earn and reinvest money. If government grows too large, it has to extract more funds from the private sector to cover public sector expenses. That means companies and individuals have less to invest in the economy, and that restricts economic growth. Thus, the tax base shrinks and the government must cut back on expenses or borrow to pay for programs. In contrast to the limit on what government can extract from the economy, the private sector has no restrictions as an engine for growth, because private corporations can tap export markets and grow as much as the global market will allow. As Anatole Kaletsky, the great economics columnist of the *London Times*, has said: "Government spending is not just unhealthy as the main driver of economic stimulus; it is also unreliable."

Of course, there's the argument that strong public sector spending benefits the overall economy because government provides infrastructure that allows businesses to operate efficiently, an education system to train present and future workers, and a health service that ensures workers are healthy and productive. It's incredibly difficult to state categorically how big the public sector should be in any given jurisdiction, but there are benchmarks that indicate a target for the Maritimes.

Let's use France as an example, again focusing on a time where there's a healthy global economy. France's government expenditures in 2007 amounted to 53.4 percent of GDP—the second highest of any member of the Organization for Economic Co-operation and Development (OECD), which is made up of the world's thirty leading economies, including many members of the European Union. There were only five OECD countries whose government expenditures exceeded 50 percent. (Canada's figure was 39.3 percent.) France's GDP growth was 2.3 percent in 2007, underperforming the European Union total of 2.8 percent, while its unemployment rate in 2007 was about 8.1 percent, exceeding the Eurozone average of 7.3 percent. Clearly, France was underperforming other European countries and had a larger public sector than almost all of them.

The only OECD country that has a larger public sector relative to its economy is Sweden with 55.5 percent. The 2007 growth rate was 4.2 percent while the 2007 unemployment rate was 5.7 percent. So a big government helps economic performance, right? Not really. Economists note that the public sector ratio for Sweden has shrunk from about 60 percent in the past decade to its current level, suggesting that jurisdictions accelerate their economic growth as they reduce the size of their government. We should also remember that Sweden's private sector is dominated by extraordinary companies such as Volvo, Ikea, Ericsson, TeliaSonera, and a range of extremely profitable financial companies. It's a technologically savvy nation, whose current account surplus amounted to 7.1 percent of GDP in 2007. (The corresponding figure for Canada, a far more resource-rich country, was 1.7 percent.) Sweden also excels at research and development, and in 2005 produced R and D spending of about 3.8 percent of GDP—tops among OECD countries. If you're going to hold up Sweden as the model of a successful economy with a large public sector, you've got to include the excellence of its private sector as the key component of that formula.

As a result, it is generally accepted—certainly among conservative economists—that Sweden is the exception rather than the rule in terms of an economic model and that jurisdictions should aim for a public sector accounting for comfortably less than half the economy. In a March 2007 speech, European Central Bank executive board member Jürgen Stark tried to calculate the perfect size of a public sector, balancing the state's need to provide services, manage its debt, and invest in infrastructure against the need for private enterprise to thrive. "We should have efficient spending that attains core social and economic objectives, but leaves us money to adapt to new challenges (such as globalization and climate change) and maintain a high quality of life," said Stark in the speech. "I would argue that 30–35 percent of GDP [devoted to the public sector] may be enough for this and it would certainly be easier to finance than the current levels of spending in many countries."

So what does this say about the Maritimes?

In 2006 (the most recent StatsCan figures available), expenditures from the three levels of government in Nova Scotia amounted to 49.7 percent of GDP. The actual figure is probably greater than that because StatsCan classifies some publicly owned enterprises as part of the private sector, and because there are other enterprises that are privately owned but work exclusively for government. The good news is the 2001 level was 51.3 percent, so the private sector was outpacing the public sector in growth during this period. But the good news ends there. Spending by the provincial government was in the 22.6–22.7 percent ballpark in both years, so there was no reduction in the provincial government as a proportion of the entire economy. In 2006, Nova Scotia had the second-highest level of public sector economic domination in Canada, exceeded only by Prince Edward Island with a level of 54.6 percent. New Brunswick came in at 47.2 percent. We are way out of whack with the rest of Canada. Because of prudent economic stewardship in the 1990s and early 2000s and the strength of resource companies, the public sector comprised 32.7 percent of the overall Canadian economy in 2006, according to StatsCan (which tabulates its figures differently than the OECD).

Consider that for a moment: Nova Scotia businesses and individuals have to devote about half of their output to the public sector while their peers in other provinces devote less than one-third. Nova Scotia is a full seventeen percentage points above the national average in this key determinant of economic growth, and New Brunswick and P.E.I. are around the same level. This is a big reason that Maritime provinces have lagged the national average in GDP growth almost every year this decade. It's impossible to think we could meet the national average in economic growth let alone exceed it given these conditions.

Of course, the large public sector could be interpreted as a benefit if Maritimers were receiving better health care, education, and other services than other provinces. But we are not. As the previous chapters indicated, the Maritimes do not have a comprehensive drug plan that other provinces have. Our universities are more expensive and our public schools underperform those of other provinces. We're about to see this problem exacerbated in Nova Scotia because in 2007, 2008, and 2009—the years since the latest StatsCan numbers on the size of the public sector—provincial government spending exceeded the growth of the overall economy.

There hasn't been strong growth in federal spending in Nova Scotia, but the province receives the mixed blessing of greater expenditure by the federal government than any other province except P.E.I. In 2006, federal spending accounted for about 34.5 percent of the Nova Scotia economy. There is one federal public servant for every 39 people in Nova Scotia, according to figures compiled by professor Tom Courchene of Queen's University. That figure is exceeded only by Prince Edward Island, with 38 people per public servant. The corresponding figures for Ontario and Alberta are 82 people and 127 people, respectively. If it sounds strange to consider federal spending a mixed blessing, remember that the Maritimes need to outperform the national average in economic growth, and that seems impossible if one-third of our economy is federal spending. First of all, with the resumption of federal deficits, spending by Ottawa is vulnerable to cuts, and second, even if federal spending does increase, it cannot increase in the long term more than the national economy.

Against this backdrop of a high concentration of federal spending, the provincial government in Nova Scotia expanded rapidly up to the recent recession. The decade leading up to the slowdown was a golden time for Nova Scotia, with low unemployment, stable growth, and strong revenue increases for the province. The government should have used that time to get its house in order. But from the end of the cutbacks in 1997–98 until the beginning of the recession in 2007–2008, the government spent excessively and unwisely. In 1997–98, the deficit-plagued Nova Scotia government budgeted $3.51 billion on programs, and that figure rose to $6.92 billion in 2007–2008—an obscene increase of 97 percent in ten years. The Halifax Regional Municipality, the largest municipality in the province, had a somewhat better record, with expenses rising about 70 percent. During the same time, inflation increased about 25 percent, and overall economic growth was also about 25 percent, which resulted in total economic growth of about 55 percent. So provincial government spending rose 97 percent and municipal spending 70 percent during a time when the economy (including inflation) grew by just over 55 percent.

If you ask someone from the government why expenses grew so quickly, the stock answer is health care costs, and they certainly were a big part of the problem. In 1997–98, the province spent $1.41 billion on health care. A decade later, the health department and the department of health promotion and protection (created in 2006) had a total budget of $3.10 billion—an increase of 122 percent. But if you look at other essential social spending such as education and community services, you get a different impression. In 1997–98, Nova Scotia had total budgets of $920 million for education and assistance to universities. Those two departments' budgets increased to a total of $1.50 billion in 2007–2008—an increase of 62 percent. Community services—the department that pays social benefits to the most disadvantaged people in society—also experienced a funding increase of 62 percent (from $548 million to $886 million) in the decade—just above the combined rise in inflation and economic growth. If we strip out these three essential departments, program spending by the Nova Scotia government rose 123 percent in the decade, from $640 million to $1.43 billion. In other words, spending on the other parts of government—energy, immigration, the public service, intergovernmental affairs, etc.—rose at the same level as health care and twice the level of education and community services. All of this happened because government spent far too much money increasing non-essential parts of its operations.

## Proliferation of Government

I define "non-essential" those specific spending categories outside of health, education, and community services that have grown vastly with little benefit to the general public. You could fill a book with them, but here are just a few egregious examples:

- *Cabinet.* When he came to office in 1999, premier John Hamm took pride in the fact that he had only eleven ministers in his cabinet, which he said was an efficient group and the smallest cabinet in recent history. "This is a province that can't afford more government," said Hamm when he shuffled his cabinet but maintained the eleven-minister total five months later. By the time he left office, Rodney MacDonald had an eighteen-member cabinet—50 percent larger than the U.S. federal government. Darrell Dexter has so far taken the Hamm line and currently has a twelve-member cabinet, though he has warned it may grow in time.

- *MLAs.* Cabinet members in 2006 earned a salary of $125,815.60, significantly more than the $80,049.21-a-year pay for the average MLA. So the large number of ministers is one reason the government revealed in November 2007 that pay and expenses for members of the legislature rose 22 percent from the previous year to $11.7 million. That increase led *Halifax Daily News* political reporter Brian Flynn to write: "The cost of politicians is rising faster than health care." Base pay for MLAs the previous year alone had risen 20 percent. The New Democrats have since frozen MLAs' pay for two years.

- *MLAs' perks.* A commission headed by former Mulroney government minister Barbara McDougall said in 2006 that there is a "deeply held conviction" in Nova Scotia that MLAs' expenses are subject to widespread abuse. In March 2007, the Internal Economy Board (a committee comprising senior cabinet ministers, the speaker, deputy speaker, and party House leaders) said there was no need to review expenses, which averaged an astonishing $208,000 per member in 2006. The New Democrats have moved to curtail some perks, such as ending the $45,000 golden handshake members receive when they leave politics.

- *Propaganda.* In 2006, at a cost of $262,000 a year, the Progressive Conservative government began mailing out a full-colour, glossy newsletter explaining what the government was doing for its citizens. Titled "What's New in Nova Scotia," the first issue had such headlines as "Creating winning conditions," "Protecting our environment," and "Healthier children, safer communities." Even local MLAs began to produce something similar: In August 2007, my MLA, Judy Streatch, distributed her own paper in her Chester–St. Margaret's riding, bearing the somewhat dubious headline: "All parties support MacDonald government." These documents were pure propaganda—and obviously failed propaganda given the government was subsequently defeated.

- *Politics as theatre.* The cost of public relations continued to escalate when the government built a small theatre in the bottom floor of Province House for about five hundred thousand dollars. The press gallery did not request such a facility, but MacDonald insisted it showcased the government as a professional organization. "What they don't seem to understand is a well-lit turkey standing in front of a line of Nova Scotia flags is still a turkey," New Democrat MLA Graham Steele told the *Chronicle Herald*.

- *Public relations.* The budget for Communications Nova Scotia was $2 million in 1998–99, but ten years later it had risen 312 percent to $8.2 million, in part because it now included the government's Come To Life program. The government had 57 spokespeople in 2000, with a top pay of $70,100, but by 2007 that number had risen to 103 PR officers with

13 making more than $70,000 a year, according to *Frank* magazine.

- *Patronage.* Former premier MacDonald rewarded people around him handsomely. Amy Smith of the *Chronicle Herald* reported in January 2009 that MacDonald's chief of staff, Bob Chisholm, received a 9.7 percent annual raise to $144,476.78 in a contract he signed October 29, 2008—at the absolute zenith of the recession. Wade Keller, the premier's director of communications, received a 15.7 percent raise in 2008 to $110,000. Earlier in the decade, communications director Dale Madill had earned an annual salary of $65,000—so this one position saw a rise of almost 70 percent in just seven years. MacDonald gave his chief of staff, Heather Foley Melvin, the job of chief administrative officer of a new office called Conserve Nova Scotia with a salary of $132,000. That appointment has been controversial, partly because Foley Melvin's title was later changed to chief executive officer—a position that should go through the proper appointment process, according to New Democrat critics. In 2008, *Frank* magazine revealed that Fred MacGillivray, the chief executive of the government-owned Trade Centre Ltd., had received an extra $800,000 pension as an inducement to stay on in his job in 2001. MacGillivray was already one of the highest paid civil servants in the province with a $202,542 annual salary plus a civil service pension, but the Trade Centre board decided he merited the extra pension. Lewis MacKinnon, an old friend of MacDonald and former Conservative federal election candidate, was named as the first chief executive officer of the office of Gaelic affairs. The post, whose role is to promote the Gaelic language, has an annual pay of $80,740.

- *Intergovernmental affairs.* This department—whose primary job is to win more money from the federal government—cost Nova Scotia $727,000 in 1997–98. That year, the province received transfers of about $1.7 billion from Ottawa, accounting for about 41 percent of the provincial revenues. In 2008–2009, the government budgeted $3.2 million on intergovernmental affairs. Since the amount spent on intergovernmental affairs has quadrupled in eleven years, you would think the amount of money Nova Scotia gets from Ottawa has quadrupled. If you've read this far, you know that's probably not the case. In 2008–2009, Nova Scotia made about $2.6 billion from the federal government, and the proportion of the revenue base that comes from Ottawa has held steady at 41 percent.

- *Crown corporation perks.* In December 2008, Chris Lambie of the *Chronicle Herald* reported that executives of the Atlantic Lotto Corporation, owned by the four Atlantic provinces, spent $549,000 over two years travelling to places like Singapore, Athens, Las Vegas, London, and Paris. The report revealed CEO Michelle Carinci incurred the most expenses. In addition to her $205,000-a-year salary, Carinci filed expense claims of $119,000 over the two-year period.

Okay, so why am I rolling this out now that the Progressive Conservatives are bug guts on the electoral windshield? First of all, it shouldn't be forgotten. The government has a penchant for paying people excessively, and the media will have to monitor whether the New Democrats maintain the practice. The NDP has preached public virtues for generations, but almost all NDP members of the legislature went along with the expense gratuities that Barbara McDougall wanted reformed. The only holdout was Graham Steele, now the finance minister. Most importantly, these examples demonstrate that there is room to make cuts in the government without jeopardizing essential services. Even a cursory view of the Nova Scotia budget documents reveals areas with huge spending increases that need to be reigned in.

There are several depressing aspects to all I've written about government largesse. First, I didn't have to look that hard to find it; it was all reported in the pages of local newspapers. There's the perception among too many people employed by the government that they are entitled to this sort of luxury and over-compensation, financed by an electorate told there's no money for road paving or universal drug coverage. It's no coincidence that it was a Nova Scotia politician, former federal cabinet minister David Dingwall, who made national headlines saying, "I am entitled to my entitlements," when he was forced out as CEO of the Royal Canadian Mint in 2005. Government officials in Nova Scotia—elected and non-elected—are too often saturated with their own sense of entitlement, and it is detrimental in a province with such an uncertain economic outlook.

Even the health department has room to cut. A senior civil servant once told me that if he was in charge and unions were prevented from striking, he could reduce the cost of the health department by 30 percent. The departments other than health, education, and community services have noble goals. It's important that Nova Scotians conserve energy and work with other Canadian governments. But the provincial government seems to operate under the assumption that it can only deal with an important issue by creating a new department or office. It's an expensive and misguided strategy, and it leads to an indisputable conclusion: holding down costs has an unacceptably low priority here.

The problem of poor cost control is exacerbated by the fragmented structure of government in the Maritimes. With the four smallest provinces in Canada, and small, proud communities that have existed for centuries, the Maritimes are an administrative mosaic, an assembly of colour chips that somehow co-exist to form a whole. But we are living in an age in which larger institutions tend to serve their citizens best. Nova Scotia's 913,000 residents are overseen by the provincial government, 55 municipalities, and 8 school boards. New Brunswick, with 730,000 people, has 108 municipal units and 14 school districts. Though it only has 135,000 people, Prince Edward Island has its own provincial legislature. But the members of this legislature obviously aren't close enough to grassroots voters because the island also has 75 municipalities, one for every 1,800 people. The smallest, Tignish Shore, has 72 people who require a local council comprising a chairperson, vice-chair, 5 councillors, and a chief administrative officer. The island also has three school boards.

Clearly, people in outlying areas like local administrations to oversee local issues, fearing that larger institutions would result in power—and therefore spending—shifting to the larger cities. But the patchwork of tiny government institutions has a cost, because we pay more for government administration than other jurisdictions do. No one can argue that the rural parts of the Maritimes have grown wealthy because of the tiny administrative bodies.

## Regional Co-operation

So there we have it. The Maritimes have more government than other parts of Canada—so much so that public expenditure comprises more than 15 percentage points more of our GDP than the rest of Canada. Nova Scotia and P.E.I. have proportionally more federal spending than any other provinces, provincial spending has been growing excessively (in large measure because of spending in non-essential areas), and there is a fragmented administration that ramps up costs and exacerbates local jealousies. The Maritimes are coping with large government at the same time as the provinces should be preparing for a chronic labour shortage due to the aging population. So what's to be done?

As I was wrapping up the final draft of this book, I realized I wasn't alone in examining the outlook for the region in these terms. Leanne Hachey of the Canadian Federation of Independent Business told me that her group was putting the finishing touches on a major report, "The Future of Atlantic Canada: Dealing with the Demographic Drought." The report, due out in the autumn of 2009, concludes that Atlantic Canada (the FDIC report includes Newfoundland and Labrador) faces a worse demographic crisis than other parts of the country, and it must therefore improve productivity and increase economic growth. That means reducing taxes and the size of the government. "We have been building up—and Nova Scotia is probably the worst—an unsustainable pattern of spending," she said. Her silver bullet for our problem is regional co-operation—combining the four provinces' government agencies and departments to cut costs. She added that the federal government may have to insist on co-operation between the four governments in order to receive federal funding for some programs. "It would be sad if it came to that level," she said, adding that it would be preferable if the four governments simply agreed among themselves to combine their various operations.

This would mark new thinking for the region, where the only true example of regional co-operation has been the dreadful Atlantic Lottery Corporation, which provides a cushy life to its executives and spreads a dubious vice that impoverishes many people. But Atlantic Lotto is profitable, so the provinces all co-operate to ensure its success. The Maritimes need to do more of this, and not just on gambling operations. Take a look at what Minnesota and Wisconsin are doing. Wisconsin governor Jim Doyle and Minnesota governor Tim Pawlenty announced plans in March 2009 to combine some services to save millions of taxpayer dollars. The two governors, one a Democrat and the other a Republican, released a 131-page report studying co-operative initiatives in virtually all departments. What caused the co-operation? Each state was facing a $5 billion deficit over the next two years and had no choice. This sort of thinking is becoming more common in the U.S. In 2007, some forty-three states participated in joint procurement programs in order to save money.

There's no limit to the agencies and departments in the Atlantic provinces that could benefit from regional co-operation. When I interviewed Darrell Dexter in July 2009, he said he liked the idea but couldn't name a department off the top of his head that could be easily merged. But I can name one now: In 2008–2009, Nova Scotia budgeted $10.3 million for Conserve Nova Scotia. Meanwhile, New Brunswick spent $12.7 million on the Energy Efficiency and Conservation Agency of New Brunswick. They do the exact same job. There's no reason they can't be combined and invite P.E.I. and possibly Newfoundland and Labrador to join them as well. It would cost less and do the exact same job as having four provinces do it on their own. Where would it be based? Doesn't matter. The region is in the early stages of a labour crunch, so it doesn't make sense to fuss about where jobs are based. Perhaps the combined energy conservation agency could be headquartered in Saint John, with the offices of the combined utilities review board in Charlottetown, the health promotion department in St. John's, and the workers' compensation board in Halifax. Or even Sydney. The details can be worked out later, but the point is that regional bureaucracy must merge because the current size of government is unsustainable given the reality of our demographics.

Essentially, Nova Scotia is going to have to change its model for economic development. Up to now, the province has been trying to grow the private and public sectors simultaneously, with the public sector leading the way and subsidizing private industry. It's a flawed plan. The major problem is that government spending in recent years actually outpaced growth in the overall economy—a thoroughly ass-backwards approach to public policy. If government is to grow, it should do so only after the private sector has increased enough to support it. British economist David Brian Smith in his book *Living with Leviathan: Public Spending, Taxes and Economic Performance* said such economic models "seem capable of generating rapid growth in their early years, when their burgeoning public spending components are boosting GDP." But, he adds, "Such economies eventually start to seize up, however, for two main reasons. The first is that investors and entrepreneurs become aware that regulatory and tax changes that affect their private returns are expropriating their capital and thus they cease to invest or take risks… Second, regulations and controls create inefficiencies, which in turn lead to more regulation and control until the whole system jams up."

Government needs to trim back spending while the private sector grows. Certainly government spending should be selective, so education, health, and capital spending can increase while programs that are preferable but not essential are eliminated or reduced. Restraint programs are great, but a 3-percent across-the-board cut to every department is not the way to do it. I'll look more closely in the next chapter at how to encourage growth in the private sector, but there's one way to shrink government and grow the private sector in one fell swoop: privatization.

## Sell Off State Assets

Privatization is the accepted means around the world for governments to transfer industry to the hands of people who will be most productive—industrialists. History shows societies grow wealthy when resources are controlled by people who can best manage the operations and apply capital to them. A case in point: fuel in England. In the fifteenth century, England was running out of trees to burn because its booming agriculture sector was cutting down forests. Coal was becoming the fuel of choice, but the Roman Catholic Church owned most of the coal-bearing land, and the church was hardly an institution to devote capital to coal mining. When Henry VIII launched the Reformation in England, he seized all church property, so the northern coalfields became state land, which were then leased to feudal landowners who had the wherewithal to develop coal mines. Eventually, the industrial revolution ensued.

Similar movements are happening now all over the world. There's no privatization in the U.S.—pretty well everything's already privately owned. Ditto Great Britain, thanks to Margaret Thatcher, whose privatization policies were continued by Tony Blair. But throughout Europe, Asia, Chile, Mexico, New Zealand, and Russia, governments are selling off state-owned industry for the benefit of government coffers and the businesses themselves. Earlier, I did a quick comparison of the economies of France and Sweden, showing how much more efficient Sweden's is despite its huge public sector. Some economists believe the reason Sweden's growth is so strong is because it has reduced the proportion of its economy controlled by the public sector through privatization. Sweden is in the middle of a privatization program that is designed to raise $21 billion over three years, including the sale of stakes in V & S, the producer of Absolut vodka; Nordea, the largest bank in the Nordic region; and TeliaSonera, the dominant telecom company in the region. France in this decade has also sold off billions of euros of assets including stakes in France Telecom, Gaz de France, and Electricité de France. I should emphasize that we're talking about the governments of France and Sweden here—the long-standing punchlines for conservatives' jokes about left-winged government. Privatization in the twenty-first century is not an evil tool wielded by Thatcherite crackpots. Within the European

Union, hundreds of billions of dollars have been raised by member states selling off government-owned assets. It's now the mainstream of economic development and is perfect for addressing the sorts of problems that the Maritimes confront.

Nova Scotia has done well in the past when it has privatized assets. In 1992, the province sold off Nova Scotia Power Inc. in an initial public offering, raising $200 million for the province and shedding $2.4 billion in debt from the provincial government's balance sheet. Just removing that debt is enough of a reason to be pleased about that privatization, but the company (now a unit of publicly listed Emera Inc.) managed to keep power rates down for almost a decade. What's more, because it's a private company, it has been able to make investments outside the province in a power company in Maine and a pipeline in New Brunswick. That means it's generating money outside the province that goes to Emera's bottom line, which then contributes corporate taxes to the Nova Scotia government. It has had its problems with power outages, and it still has to contend with the legacy of coal-fired plants. The stock has been a dog in terms of performance, gaining 10 percent in ten years, and the only reason to hold it is for dividend income. But it's difficult to believe that NSPC would be a better company today if it were still owned by our debt-ridden government. The privatization of the Nova Scotia utility brings to mind the obvious need to privatize New Brunswick Power, a company with $1.2 billion in annual revenue. Such a move would lower New Brunswick's debt, produce another publicly traded company in the region, and give the privatized company the ability to seek new markets, as Emera has done.

What assets could be privatized now in Nova Scotia? Lots. I'd leave the Nova Scotia Liquor Commission in public hands (because a debate about its privatization would be dominated by social, not economic, issues), but there are other businesses that belong in private hands. Nova

Scotia now owns three wonderful hotel/resort complexes—Keltic Lodge in Ingonish, Liscombe Lodge in Guysborough County, and Digby Pines in Digby. I've stayed at each and they're fantastic. But there's no reason they should be owned by the government. The province brought in a private management company to operate them five years ago, but that doesn't go far enough. They should be sold, in whole or in part. That would allow a new Nova Scotia hotel company to grow and possibly expand outside the province, bringing revenues into the province. The argument that they couldn't be run as profitable companies is pure hogwash—certainly the Inverary Resort in Baddeck and Oak Island and White Point resorts on the South Shore can make a go of it.

The Nova Scotia government now owns twelve thousand housing units for seniors and people who need subsidized housing. There's a lot of upkeep needed in this aging housing stock. In 2006, the government admitted that more than two-thirds of these units were at least twenty-five years old, and many of them needed substantial work. The province in 2009 announced it will spend $133 million to improve its housing infrastructure, which will include repairs to the older stock. I have no way of knowing whether this expenditure is simply a finger-in-the-dyke remedy, but I do know the province will need more money again in a few years, and again a few years after that, to constantly upgrade public housing units. There's a better way to do it. The government should be giving people who live in public housing the option of buying their homes—especially the ones that have just been repaired. The government could offer them at an attractive price, to minimize any downside risk the residents might face. The money raised by the government could upgrade other properties, or build long-term care facilities for seniors. It's been done before. "Perhaps Margaret Thatcher, of all people, suggested a program that might help," wrote British historian Niall Ferguson in his 2008 book *The Ascent of Money: A Financial History of the World*, in discussing public housing. "In the 1980s, she turned 1.5 million residents of public housing projects in Britain into homeowners. It was certainly the most liberal thing Mrs. Thatcher did, and perhaps progressives should borrow a leaf from her playbook." Perhaps they should. Sadly, this is Nova Scotia and privatization is rarely debated.

One asset that I find intriguing is the Halifax–Dartmouth Bridge Commission. I know people in Dartmouth would like to see this body disbanded so the bridges could be accessed free of charge like any other road or bridge. But the commission poses a wonderful opportunity to create a Nova Scotia–based infrastructure company. The numbers are mouth-watering. In 2007, the commission's revenue was $27.0 million—a rise of 4.4 percent over the previous year. That growth isn't bad, but what's exciting is the profit margin. The commission made a profit of $6.5 million, for a profit margin of a whopping 24 percent. The bridge commission would be a small company, with only two aging bridges as assets, but it might achieve a valuation of twenty times earnings, which would give it a value of $130 million. It's not a big company, but it's a start. This is a corporation with solid cash flow, a stable base, and a marketable piece of technology in its MacPass electronic payment system. What is the company doing in the hands of the Nova Scotia government?

I'm not the only one who believes the bridge commission should be privatized. Jamie Baillie, the president and CEO of the Atlantic Credit Union and a former chief of staff to then-Premier John Hamm, has said publicly that the Maritime provinces' public pension funds should invest in such businesses as the bridge commission and other infrastructure projects. Baillie believes—correctly—that such funding could provide stable, long-term growth for pension holders and capital for projects within the Maritimes. I think he's on the right track, though the auction of public assets like the bridge commission should not be restricted to local investors. Any credible investors should be allowed to invest in these assets to bring capital into the province and help the government reduce its debt. But whenever I've discussed this with provincial officials, they've given me a rather pathetic look and carefully explained that their first duty is to the pension holders and therefore choose—and I'm not making this up—the security of the stock and bond markets. Kind of makes you wonder how we got that $2.4 billion pension fund gap, doesn't it?

I don't think it's unreasonable to expect the Nova Scotia government could raise $500 million in proceeds in a privatization program spanning a few years. New Brunswick could undoubtedly raise even more because it could sell off its electricity company. The downside is that there's execution risk, meaning any privatized company could end up being badly run. Privatization could raise less money than expected, and there's the loss of patronage plums for the governing party. Political parties love to reward their grandees with directorships on Crown corporations like the bridge commission, trade centre, or the Waterfront Development Corporation. That would vanish if such bodies were privatized. For some, that would be a bad thing. For the region overall, it would be as good for us as privatization programs have been for Sweden.

As far as Nova Scotia goes, I can't see the NDP taking the lead in a privatization program. It's not in their genetic makeup. When I spoke to Darrell Dexter about the subject in 2009, he seemed unimpressed. The bridge commission was a public works asset and wouldn't be touched. He did indicate the Waterfront Development Corporation properties are not being held by the province in perpetuity, so maybe there will be some movement there. But even if the NDP government privatized everything it could get its hands on, it would only be one component in a broader attempt to grow the private sector.

# *private sector*

I've established that Nova Scotia has an exceedingly large public sector by Canadian and international standards, and that a jurisdiction with such a high concentration of government will likely underperform its competitors with larger private enterprise. So to reach the goal of exceeding overall Canadian economic growth, the province is going to have to grow the private sector and shrink the government. In the Maritimes' current situation, any discussion of economic development can only mean growing private enterprise—growing institutions, non-governmental organizations, or the government itself simply won't do it.

This is not to say that businesses in the Maritime Provinces do not need government support. The evidence indicates that young ventures in the region need some sort of support, whether in the form of mentoring, marketing, subsidies, or just plain encouragement. The sad fact is that this is one of the worst places in North America to start a small business, according to a report released by the Fraser Institute in December 2007. The Vancouver-based think tank evaluated the number of small businesses started in each province in Canada and state in the U.S. in 2002–2003, then compared it with the number that went belly up in the same time. It concluded that Nevada, Florida, and Utah offered the best environments for entrepreneurs, because the number of new businesses so greatly exceeded the number of failures. At the other end of the spectrum, the five worst jurisdictions in North America were the four Atlantic provinces and Saskatchewan. "Saskatchewan, Nova Scotia, New Brunswick, and Prince Edward Island recorded negative net business creation—meaning they actually lost businesses over the time period studied," said the report. It did not say why the Maritime provinces has such a poor record in starting and perpetuating small ventures, but it's probably the reasons we've already discussed: small, fragmented markets, high taxes, high energy costs, and a lack of qualified personnel. The report did note that the creation of small businesses is a key factor in future economic growth, because young, growing companies regenerate their investments, providing jobs for young people and creating wealth for their investors. It's clearly an area in which the Maritimes must do a better job.

Even by late 2008, the Fraser Institute still turned thumbs down on the Maritimes' overall business conditions. Nova Scotia scored 3.3 out of 10, narrowly beating out P.E.I.'s Canada-worst score of 3.1. New Brunswick came in seventh-worst with a score of 3.7. The study examined corporate and personal income tax, fiscal prudence, transportation infrastructure, corporate capital tax, labour regulation, and regulatory burden. The lone bright spot was that Nova Scotia topped the ranking in transportation infrastructure. Though one provincial official dismissed the study as being out of touch with the modern economy, it highlights once again how difficult it is to develop businesses in Eastern Canada. The good news is that the Nova Scotia government has two fantastic bodies for developing businesses—Nova Scotia Business Inc., the government's arm's-length bridge to the business community; and InNOVAcorp, a semi-autonomous agency that acts as incubator, mentor, and sometimes venture capital backer to innovative young companies.

InNOVAcorp helps young companies develop products, software, and services for the global economy in three ways. First, it provides advice to entrepreneurs so they can move from the research stage to producing products and services that people will buy. Second, it provides research facilities, including office and lab space in Halifax and Dartmouth. Finally, it takes equity positions in companies it believes have superb prospects. InNOVAcorp is so good at what it does that the National Business Incubation Association of Athens, Ohio, which has almost two thousand members in sixty-six countries, awarded the agency a silver medal in its 2009 international competition for business incubators. The only incubator better than our own InNOVAcorp was San Jose BioCenter in Silicon Valley. "We have a unique model," says Dan MacDonald, the agency's president and CEO. "Around North America you'll find lots of incubators, but they're real estate plays mainly, providing an office or a lab. There may be some mentoring, but almost never do you find the investment that we put into the companies."

These investments are not subsidies but venture capital investments in private companies. Access to such venture capital investments is desperately needed to develop a knowledge economy, and it's an area where the Maritime region is sorely lacking. Venture capital firms take small stakes in young companies, hoping a few of them prosper. According to Thomson Financial, nine Nova Scotia companies received a total of twenty-four million dollars in venture capital (VC) financing in 2006, up from seven investments worth seventeen million dollars a year earlier. (I'm choosing 2006 because it was a particularly good year for Nova Scotia, and VC everywhere began to fall off in 2007.) Yet that 2006 figure accounted for a mere 1.4 percent of the Canadian total. Nova Scotia has about 3 percent of the country's population, but draws in just 1.4 percent of its venture capital financing in a good year. One reason Nova Scotia does so poorly is there are no large VC firms based in the region, so Nova Scotia does not benefit from the localized nature of this business. Wayne Bussey, president and chief executive of Telecom Applications Research Alliance, a Halifax-based group dedicated to developing tech companies, says one problem with raising funds in the Maritimes is VC investors prefer investing in their own backyard. Nova Scotia, P.E.I., and Newfoundland and Labrador are now the only provinces without alternative investment segments in their public pension funds. New Brunswick has taken some steps in the right direction. The province authorized the New Brunswick Investment Management Corp., which manages public sector pensions, to channel a small portion of its funds into VC investments. It's also let it be known it would gladly merge with other Atlantic Canadian pension funds, but no other province has accepted. One public sector pension group for all the Maritimes, even if based in New Brunswick, would best serve its contributors and the regional economy.

InNOVAcorp itself ameliorates this sorry situation by providing a local partner for out-of-town VC funds. Dan MacDonald explained in a 2009 interview that the agency's Nova Scotia First Fund has invested seven million dollars in various companies between 2003 and 2009. But those investments in turn have lured in other investors, so a total of twenty-five million dollars was invested in the provincial economy.

In the dying days of the Tory government, Dan MacDonald received approval to expand the Nova Scotia First Fund with a commitment of thirty million dollars over ten years. The agency also became a limited partner in the eighty-million-dollar Cycle Capital Fund I LP, a Montreal clean-tech fund. The plan is to participate in the fund and encourage it to direct money into some of the exciting clean-tech companies sprouting up in Nova Scotia. What's great about this endeavour is that, by participating in national and international entities, MacDonald is moving beyond the petty parochialism that hamstrings this economy.

There's another provincial program that has done a good job of channelling small amounts of money into young businesses. Pioneered in Nova Scotia, Community Economic Development Investment Funds, or Cedifs, began in 1999 as a means of directing Registered Retirement Savings Program (RRSP) money into local communities. Basically, the Cedif program allows community-based groups to form ventures and seek investment from local contributors, who can then place the investments in their RRSPs. The program has raised about twenty-five million dollars in Nova Scotia communities through forty-one offerings— nothing that will arrest the decline of rural economies, but certainly an encouraging development. The remarkably simple and effective program is now raising about five million dollars annually, and has been especially effective in raising money for wind farms. (The Nova Scotia government frequently says Cedifs are necessary because RRSPs withdraw about six hundred million dollars from Atlantic Canada and less than 2 percent of this is reinvested in the region. That's a bit rich, given that the provincial government's employee pension plan refuses to participate in local VC, private equity, or infrastructure investments, preferring instead the "security" of listed businesses for civil servants' pensions.)

The main shortcoming of InNOVAcorp and Cedifs is that they don't have the firepower to make significant follow-on investments, restricting the competitive abilities of the companies they invest in. According to Thomson Financial, the average VC investment in Canadian companies in 2006 was about $4.2 million, less than half the $10.1 million figure reported for the U.S. In Nova Scotia, the average investment was $2.7 million, and that was considered a good year. "We need to be able to invest more in our companies," said Toon Nagtegaal, the chief executive of Wave Venture Partners of Lunenburg. "We cannot expect our entrepreneurs, who are at a disadvantage to start with because they have to export what they produce, to compete against companies who have more money than they do."

## Nova Scotia Business Inc.

Part of the gap in funding for corporations is filled by Nova Scotia Business Inc. (NSBI), the other provincial agency set up to help develop the private sector. NSBI also has an impressive venture capital portfolio, but its primary function is attracting businesses to the province and providing subsidies that allow offshore and domestic businesses to grow. The agency has a higher profile than InNOVAcorp, and its CEO, Stephen Lund, is often sought out by the media as the government's spokesperson on economic and development issues. Forthright and forceful, Lund operates a tight shop, and even says with a straight face that NSBI is part of the private, not public, sector. That's a stretch given that all its funding comes from the government. But you could argue that NSBI acts like a private enterprise in that it actively courts business rather than waiting for clients (NSBI calls them clients) to come calling.

NSBI's crowning achievement was convincing Research in Motion Ltd. to establish a $230-million technical support office in Halifax, creating about 1,250 jobs. Halifax was not really on the Waterloo, Ontario-based BlackBerry-maker's radar screen, but Lund and his team cold-called the company, even convincing premier John Hamm to fly to Waterloo to meet with RIM's senior management. When the province finally announced the deal in November 2005, the ceremony at Pier 21 in Halifax had the atmosphere of a tickertape parade. The audience of about four hundred included former premier Gerald Regan and IMP Group founder Ken Rowe. When Lund finally announced RIM chairman and co-CEO Jim Balsillie, he might as well have been introducing the Rolling Stones. The hall erupted into the first of three standing ovations for the RIM honcho. "There's not a jurisdiction in the world who wouldn't love to be here now," said Lund, beaming with joy. Truer words were never spoken. Lund and his crew had bagged the biggest beast in the jungle.

Nova Scotia Business Inc. scored again a year later when it announced in quick succession that four financial companies with links to Bermuda would set up offices in Halifax, joining West End Capital, which had made a similar announcement a year earlier. The financial companies never quite generated the volcanoes of ecstasy that erupted over RIM, but the story of their entry to Nova Scotia demonstrates how NSBI works. From 1991 to 1996, Lund had worked in Bermuda for Butterfield Bank, so he was familiar with the potential and problems of that sunny little tax haven. It has potential because it is a low-tax jurisdiction with a burgeoning cluster of offshore financial businesses, especially hedge funds and insurers. Its problem is that it is small, expensive, and its businesses have a hell of a time attracting and retaining workers. So Lund and his team came up with a plan. They proposed courting Bermuda financial companies to let them know they could establish back offices in Halifax, which has direct flights to Bermuda, lower costs than the island,

and (theoretically) a vast pool of talent that could be restocked by the province's thriving community of business schools. Lund dispatched J. P. Robicheau, a business development executive with NSBI, to the island to cold-call financial firms and ascertain what they needed in terms of human resources and infrastructure. Then they began to invite managers from these companies to visit Halifax and see what the city had to offer.

Under the leadership of NSBI and the Greater Halifax Partnership, Halifax has learned a thing or two about how to behave when corporate elite comes to town. They know that visiting businesspeople want to learn about Halifax's strengths—its quality of life, its workforce, and its universities. These visitors often ask to meet representatives of the universities, if possible. So local organizers like to begin these one-day visits with an early meeting with the presidents of three or four universities and the Nova Scotia Community College—all in the same room, at the same time. NSBI constantly hears from these visiting businesspeople that they were expecting to visit one university and then another. By getting all the leading educators together, the company considering a move to Halifax can ask all education-related questions at once and get an understanding of how the province's universities co-operate with business, government, and each other. Then the organizers take the foreign businesspeople to meet members of the local business community and see facilities that pertain to their business—the downtown, the research labs, the port, the airport. They like to cap the day off with a banquet with business, academic, and government leaders, and have been known to hold these dinners at Citadel Hill, attended to by cadets in full Highland uniform. The results are not always successful—the Indian industrial giant Tata Group was given the full treatment, but nothing came of it—but the approach helped in securing the five financial companies.

NSBI is not universally adored in the business community or government. Some businesses believe NSBI is so bedazzled by international companies that it ignores the needs of Nova Scotia enterprises. Lund also gets criticism from people outside Halifax for focusing too much on the capital, but there is plenty of evidence that foreign companies want to set up shop in Halifax rather than a satellite community simply because it is the best place for business in Nova Scotia. Yet NSBI has an impressive track record in spite of strong competition from similar bodies in every Canadian province and U.S. state. One final thing about NSBI, which is a little-known boon for Nova Scotia—it contains its costs. It began life in the 2001–2002 fiscal year with a budget of $29.4 million and its budget for 2007–2008 is $26.6 million.

Based on their successes, InNOVAcorp and NSBI should be the cornerstones of economic development in Nova Scotia in the coming years. Better still, if regional co-operation takes hold, they should change their name to shed their Nova Scotia bias and extend their reach to New Brunswick and P.E.I. Even in their current form, both agencies have a more distinguished track record than the economic development department (now economic and rural development), which has overseen the problematic Industrial Expansion Fund and undergone the type of bureaucratic bloating that plagued the MacDonald government. This department always seems to be in a state of flux, changing its name four times in eleven years, its budget expanding and often being overspend (by almost 50 percent in 1999–2000 alone). In the past five years, the department's budget has had annual increases of 25.5 percent, 16.7 percent, 32.8 percent, 27.0 percent, and 20.0 percent. Its budget has almost tripled in five years. Why has it expanded? Certainly it hands out more subsidies than before, but the bureaucracy has also grown. Consider, for example, the economic strategies and initiatives division, which "provides research, analysis, leadership, and support for the development processes underpinning implementation of government's initiatives in economic development, innovation, and technology." Its budget rose 450 percent in two years to $16.5 million in 2007–2008 from $3.0 million in 2005–2006. Once again, we're seeing massive increases in discretionary spending. "We keep saying to them, 'If you're looking for some place to cut spending, start there,'" said Leanne Hachey, referring to the economic development budget.

Of course, businesspeople have never been known to complain about the Industrial Expansion Fund, which the department oversees. In 2007–2008, for example, the grants and contributions exceeded the budget by about one-third, and the department ended up handing out $80.7 million—three times the budget of NSBI. The way the economic development department has handed out money to the private sector is a problem—historically, it's been deeply politicized and often based on regional loyalties. The use of the fund sparked a political scandal in 2005 when the government lent $250,000 to S and J Potato Farms, which, it turned out, leased land from then-economic development minister Ernie Fage. When the scandal broke, Fage resigned his cabinet seat. (He later re-entered cabinet, only to resign in disgrace again.) Another $350,000 of industrial expansion money was lent to Magic Valley Family Fun Park, owned by friends of then-premier John Hamm. Businesses that have contributed to the ruling party seem to do very well from the fund. In fact, the *Daily News* of Halifax reported that the office of economic development handed money to thirteen businesses in 2004, and nine of them had made political contributions to the Nova Scotia Progressive Conservatives. The contributors included Crossley Carpet Mills Ltd., which donated $2,339 over two years to the Tories and received $1.5 million from the fund in 2004. The French tire-maker Michelin SA, which has two plants in Nova Scotia, gave the Tories $10,000 in 2003 and received $4 million from the province in 2004.

The government has tightened rules on financial contributions to political parties, so this is likely to be less of a problem in the future. But there is still something annoying about the way government and businesspeople have helped each other out over the years. Governments have always been willing to repay political contributions with grants and loans to businesses, but what's odd is businesspeople have rarely been able to use their political clout to convince the government to bring in meaningful reforms that improve the overall economy.

So what reforms are needed to allow private companies to thrive?

As I've already stated, the government should adopt an aggressive privatization program. Then it should expand its Public-Private Partnerships, or P3, and adopt a robust program of deregulation, negotiate with Alberta and British Columbia to join their TILMA, publicly support the aims of the Atlantica movement, and develop policies to increase the growth of Halifax as the commercial centre for the region.

After years of being horrified by the thought, Nova Scotia government in 2008 began to adopt P3 financing. A common practice around the world, public-private partnerships allow private companies to participate in public development, such as building a hospital or a school, for a profit. Sometimes the government will lease the facility from the contractor, sometimes the contractor charges end-users for the use of the facility, such as with a toll road. The Liberal government adopted the program in the 1990s to build schools, and the project ended up with cost overruns of almost 10 percent and only about 60 percent of the required schools were built. That contributed to the lingering impression in some circles that P3 projects don't work, that private companies tend to fleece the government, and that public projects are best left to government. The government of the day admitted that provincial bureaucrats did a poor job of site selection and monitoring the programs, and other commentators have said the contracts were badly written. If it's done properly (such as the Confederation Bridge to P.E.I.), the citizens end up with a top-flight facility while the government avoids burdensome capital investment.

The MacDonald government tiptoed back into P3 programs late in its tenure, though it called them "strategic infrastructure partnerships." The government sought advice—for two hundred thousand dollars—from Victoria, B.C.-based Partnerships British Columbia Inc. on the best way to proceed with ten projects that could be carried out as P3 developments. They include replacing or upgrading a major hospital in Halifax and upgrading the Trans-Canada Highway in the northeastern mainland. The big question, of course, is what the New Democrats will do now that they're in power in Nova Scotia. Darrell Dexter speaks eloquently about the need to develop an entrepreneurial spirit in Nova Scotia to keep young people employed here. His party has inherited a province with a huge need for infrastructure upgrades with minimal public sector costs. So he and finance minister Graham Steele may lead their cabinet to embrace P3. It will take remarkable courage, given their colleagues who have lined up against it. One other factor at play is that the sewage systems in Halifax that malfunctioned and stunk up the city were P3 projects. As well as remarkable courage, it will take some bold leadership (and ironclad contracts) to promote P3 in Nova Scotia.

## Untangle Regulations

Nova Scotia also has to do more to untangle its labyrinth-like world of business regulations. Businesspeople cannot understand why there's not a greater move to remove or amend them. It would cost the government very little and would improve the economy. Analyzing regulation is difficult because there is no real theme to the patchwork of rules that overlay the economy. There is one silly rule here and another one there. Some are well known, such as rules on Sunday shopping that were in place until 2006.

For example, Nova Scotia is the only province to ban uranium mining (though the government is reviewing that policy). Gasoline prices are regulated. Beer cannot be sold at corner stores as it can in most other provinces. Businesses must be re-registered each year. The intricate planning guidelines for downtown Halifax drive some developers away in frustration, and can tie a project up for years with a series of appeals. Teachers licensed in other provinces can't transfer here automatically. There are complexities in building codes and building inspections that even developers cannot comprehend. These are just a few of the regulations that apply within Nova Scotia. Then there are the differences in regulations among the Maritime provinces, which greatly exacerbate these problems.

Sunday shopping is a perfect example of how silly rules harm the economy and are hell to erase. By October 2004, when the province held a referendum on the issue, Nova Scotia was the only province in Canada that banned Sunday shopping. In the referendum, about 55 percent of Nova Scotians chose to maintain the ban, though a majority of those in metro Halifax wanted to end it. The ban remained across the entire province, even though opponents estimated it cost the provincial economy nineteen million dollars a year. The governing Tories' political strength was in rural counties, and they had no wish to offend their constituents. Only when Sobeys and Loblaws took the province to court and opened stores in violation of the ban in August 2006 did the government cave in. What is particularly worrying about the issue is that the economic argument was given such a low priority by the general population. The data supplied through this book demonstrates that Nova Scotia is lagging North America economically, and it is affecting our quality of life—not just the money we earn but our ability to pay for health care and education. But 55 percent of the province's voters—who received no leadership from the government—felt it was more important to have a traditional day of rest than to improve the economy. It's difficult to see how the province can exceed our competitors when the general population attaches so little importance to economic issues.

The Sunday shopping debacle was not an isolated incident. In September 2006, NSBI boss Stephen Lund warned in an interview I conducted for the *Globe and Mail* that the plan to establish Halifax as a financial services centre was being jeopardized by the shortage of grade-A office space in downtown Halifax. Financial companies don't want to settle in suburban business parks, nor in older buildings in a downtown core. They demand downtown grade-A space. According to data from CB Richard Ellis Ltd, Halifax's core grade-A vacancy rate fell to 3.9 percent in the second quarter of 2006. "What keeps me awake at night is we don't have any office space," said Lund in the interview. "I'm not sure we could accommodate another Citco here right now." Yet as of the summer of 2009, almost three years later, we still have not seen new office space under construction, and there have been unfortunate examples of good projects being delayed by heritage concerns. (I'm not a ferocious opponent of the Heritage Trust. I agree with them more buildings should be preserved. They have been correct over the years to call for more residential development in the city centre, and Barrington Street would look less like a war zone if we had it. But I do think they've picked their battles badly and their credibility has been damaged.) The classic example is the fight over the Armour Group's sixteen-million-dollar, nine-storey Waterside Centre development, which would have demolished the bulk of four heritage buildings while preserving their facades. HRM council failed to approve the project, which was then tied up in appeals before the Nova Scotia Utility and Review Board. The board ultimately allowed the project to proceed. HRMbyDesign, which HRM had assigned the task of planning development, is aiming to implement new rules that will end these sorts of appeals, but only time will tell.

Another province has proven that unravelling the network of regulations is possible. British Columbia, one of the richest provinces in Canada, decided in 2001 that overregulation was damaging its economy, so it established a special office of deregulation. The government was struck by the time and effort businesses and individuals— society as a whole, really—expended adhering to the various regulations. It was also struck by the success of Ireland in reducing businesses' administrative burden, and the economic benefits that produced. "The economic performance of this province will be significantly impacted by how successful we become at creating a regulatory environment that facilitates economic activity, while protecting the public interest," the government concluded. At the time, B.C. had 382,139 regulations, and the new office of deregulation was charged with reducing that number by one-third in three years. By 2004, it had removed 37 percent of those regulations from its books. The office then began its next phase of deregulation, which was an effort to improve the quality of regulations. It continues to carry out this work.

British Columbia can also provide us with an example of how to improve the business environment by co-operating with neighboring provinces. Alberta and British Columbia together have 7.9 million citizens and a combined gross domestic product in 2006 of $303 billion, or $38,354 per person. It's worth a mention that they are two of the four fastest-growing economies in Canada. (The three Maritime provinces have 1.8 million people and a total gross domestic product of $51.1 billion, or $30,054 per person. As we've seen, the three Maritime provinces in any given year are jogging at the back of the pack in the growth sweepstakes.) Despite the strong performance of their economies, the leaders of Alberta and B.C. believed their businesses were operating in too small a domestic market. As I've mentioned previously, these two governments signed an agreement to ensure the complete movement of trade, investment, and labour between their provinces—the Alberta–B.C. Trade, Investment and Labour Mobility Agreement, or TILMA. In other words, if you can sell any product or service in one province, you can sell it in the other. There are no barriers to investment. Anyone who can legally work in one province can cross the border and work in the other without requalifying, and there is a financial penalty if either province breaks the rules. In theory, such rules exist across Canada as the premiers of all the provinces signed the Agreement on Internal Trade in 1994, hoping to open domestic trade, but critics say the earlier agreement does not go far enough. It does not allow the complete mobility of labour and imposes no financial penalties. For example, Quebec prohibits the sale of margarine that's the same colour as butter in an effort to protect dairy farmers, and in 2005 the panel overseeing interprovincial trade complaints ruled that Quebec had to end the ban. The weird orangey hue of Quebec margarine remains to this day, but there has been no penalty imposed. Provincial premiers have said that they will soon come up with an enforceable mechanism for settling interprovincial trade disputes, but there's no shortage of skeptics.

Businesspeople in Atlantic Canada—Nova Scotia and elsewhere—like the Alberta–B.C. TILMA and want something similar in these parts. What they disagree on is how to bring it about. The Greater Halifax Partnership, for example, is calling for at least two of the larger Atlantic provinces to form an East Coast TILMA modelled on the Alberta–B.C. agreement, with the hope of eventually having all four provinces sign on. "I can't think of a better living example of how it can be done," said Brad Smith, until recently the vice-president of business development at the partnership. "In a world market, they have recognized the importance of co-operation and Atlantic Canada has to do the same thing." However, Ian Munro, the director of research at the Halifax-based Atlantic Institute of Market Studies, says the creation of an East Coast bloc runs the risk of replacing provincial trade zones with regional zones, and would expend a lot of time and resources without fully solving the problem of fragmented markets. The think tank is advocating that at least one Atlantic province negotiate to join the Western group in hopes the others will follow.

So far, none of the Atlantic provinces have taken any steps toward either plan, with some saying they would prefer to work through the Council of the Federation (as the premiers' group is now known) rather than through regional deals. "There appears to be wide support in the business community…urging us to join [the bloc] or form a regional [pact]," Greg Bent, Nova Scotia's provincial trade representative, the top civil servant on the subject, said in 2007. "We're watching the implementation of [the agreement] pretty closely."

A TILMA would be important because currently too many businesses are hampered by the tiny, fragmented markets in the region. One example would be labour-sponsored venture capital funds. I've established that the region's businesses need more capital, especially follow-on capital, from venture capital investors. Labour-sponsored VC pools can help address this need by allowing ordinary people to sink their RRSP investments into funds that could make venture capital investments. But there's a catch: provincial rules dictate that all money raised in a province have to be invested in that province. Actually there's another catch: Prince Edward Island has different rules than Nova Scotia and New Brunswick. These rules even extend to advertising, so a labour-sponsored VC fund that is launching a campaign in the region has to have different ads in P.E.I. than in the other two provinces, driving up the costs of fundraising. People in the VC business say the region also loses out because no one can form a regional fund large enough to make decent follow-on investments in Maritime businesses. That means growing Maritime businesses have more difficulty in raising capital than their competitors in other parts of North America.

## Maritimers, Unite!

For all that Maritimers like each other, the region has a pathetic record of working together. Rather than co-operating in developing a sound economic policy for the benefit of all, the history of the region's development has been marked by petty squabbles and counterproductive bickering. The history of the pipeline carrying Sable Island gas to New England is just one of myriad examples. In 2002, New Brunswick went to the National Energy Board to oppose the pipeline, claiming the project was tapping export markets while ignoring the need for natural gas in local markets. Prince Edward Island joined the New Brunswick opposition, which the NEB overruled. In 2006, Rodney MacDonald openly protested against Halifax-based Emera Inc. building a pipeline from the proposed LNG terminal in Saint John through New Brunswick to the U.S. border. Though he did not formally oppose the project before the NEB, MacDonald complained that the project could make two Nova Scotia LNG projects less likely to proceed. Thus, all three Maritime provinces this decade have shown complete ignorance of the fact that they all benefit when these projects proceed. We are each other's main trading partners and when one province grows wealthier the benefits spill over to other provinces. New Brunswick is doing splendidly from the development of energy, and it was ridiculous to oppose energy developments in their infancy. It's unbelievable to think the premier of Nova Scotia opposed a Nova Scotia company's project, which will feed profits back to the Halifax headquarters, where the Nova Scotia government will tax them.

The lack of co-operation between the provinces is one reason the Nova Scotia government should take an assertive role in supporting the Atlantica movement. Atlantica presents a low-pain opportunity for the governments of Atlantic Canada to improve living standards, and it's an opportunity that is being sadly missed. Atlantica is essentially an effort to create a trade bloc comprising the Atlantic provinces, the south shore of the St. Lawrence River in Quebec, northern New York state, and the New England states north of Massachusetts. The theory—founded on the most fundamental of economic thinking—is that if these jurisdictions adopt the same regulations and allow the movement of goods and services across the whole area, then the economies would improve. So far, the greatest political leadership on the issue has come from municipalities while the provinces have all but ignored it. "Atlantica is a divisive issue," said New Brunswick premier Shawn Graham when I asked him about it. It does not have to be. The opponents of Atlantica are largely well-intentioned but ill informed anti-globalization protestors, and the people responsible for nurturing our economy should have the courage to point out the flaws in their arguments.

Atlantica advocates are simply pushing for harmonized regulations across the region. For example, one of the key goals of the Atlantica movement is to establish a trucking corridor from Nova Scotia to Buffalo to encourage the shipment of goods throughout the bloc. But there are different trucking regulations in the different jurisdictions. Maine and New Brunswick, for example, have different weight requirements and specifications for trucks, so truckers have to drop loads at the border and make expensive adjustments. A simple harmonization of the rules would solve the problem, but there has been no movement—none. The Canadian Centre for Policy Alternatives denounced the proposed trucking policy, saying it would benefit a few areas while failing to address the needs of the rest of the Atlantic provinces. The centre also said the plan to use Halifax as a transit point for Asian goods ignores plans to expand the Panama Canal by 2015 and heightened U.S. border security. "Atlantica is not about increasing trade within the region," concluded CCPA senior researcher Scott Sinclair. "It is about convincing Atlantic Canadians that the road to prosperity lies in becoming a conduit for Asian goods headed to the American 'heartland' and in accelerating energy exports to the U.S."

Where to begin on that one? The Atlantica concept definitely promotes increasing trade across this defined bloc, including selling more energy and facilitating the movement of Asian goods to the U.S. That certainly sounds to me like a plan to increase trade. Energy and transportation are simply two industries that would benefit. The Atlantica concept is about increasing the size of the region's domestic market, and while the Port of Halifax, the trucking industry, and energy industries would benefit, so would the myriad other industries in the region because they would be operating in a larger market. Atlantica would require no additional government spending and would threaten few sacred cows in government bureaucracies. It's an absolute economic no-brainer, and it has gone nowhere, likely because it involves co-operation with parts of the U.S. and its opponents simply don't like the U.S. Since the proposal was put forward in the late 1990s, it has gained supporters in various business communities. The Atlantic Provinces Chamber of Commerce even appointed an American, Jonathan T. T. Daniels, the executive director of the Port of Oswego Authority in upstate New York, as its chair. Several city mayors have been pushing the Atlantica concept. But it has excited two powerful (if irrational) emotions among the political left—the fear of globalization and anti-American bigotry. Thus no provincial government has embraced it, and in the absence of political leadership, it has become the subject of a cat fight between the CCPA and the anti-globalization movement on one hand, and the business community on the other. The Maritimes need political leadership strong enough to articulate the economic axiom that our economy will benefit if we enlarge our market.

There's one final element that will increase our economic growth: a recognition that the economic engine is Halifax. There's a constant debate going on in government circles about whether development efforts should focus on building businesses where they have the greatest chance of succeeding or where they are most needed. Inevitably, this becomes a Halifax versus everyone else debate. The Nova Scotia legislature is dominated by rural ridings, so the greatest emphasis has been placed on halting or slowing the decline of rural areas, which is understandable but regrettable. It's understandable because parts of rural Nova Scotia are going through tough times. In 2007 alone, the TrentonWorks railcar plant in Pictou County was shuttered, throwing 350 people out of work, as was the Seafreez fish plant in Canso, affecting 200 workers. Early in the year, Maple Leaf Foods closed its fresh poultry-processing facility in

Canard, tossing about 380 people out of work. Even the urban parts of Cape Breton are suffering through a prolonged economic drought, with an unemployment rate above 17 percent as of the summer of 2009. The situation in Cape Breton is so desperate and unending that the Cape Breton Regional Municipality's staff prepared a discussion paper in July 2009 examining the future of the island and raising the prospects of Cape Breton breaking away from the rest of Nova Scotia. Obviously these problems can't be ignored.

So the government's policies are largely designed to fight a rearguard action against rural decline. Grants to rural development bodies increased from nothing in 2005–2006 to an estimated $8.6 million two years later. A large part of the industrial expansion fund goes to rural companies— gas regulation was originally proposed as a means of saving rural gas stations. The policy is regrettable because economists firmly believe the best way to develop a modern economy is to develop a "hub" city. Halifax is the hub for the Maritime region. So if Halifax is the centre with the best resources, broadest range of skilled employees, and most effective administrative and distribution operations, then economic policy should work on building up that concentrated mass of businesses. It is, after all, the place where businesses will have the greatest chance of success. As they grow, the benefits of the commercial hub radiate outward as the successful companies buy goods from the surrounding hinterland.

The provincial capital today is Nova Scotia's greatest economic asset, largely because of its workforce, universities, and the fact it's a great place to live. It has a vibrant arts community, which development guru Richard Florida lists as a criterion for strong economic growth, a thriving technology sector, and the second-highest proportion of financial services workers of any city in Canada, lagging only Toronto. The aerotech industry, led by Kenneth Rowe's IMP Group Ltd., is flourishing.

Downtown Halifax is the financial centre of the region and Burnside Industrial Park its distribution centre. In fact, in 2007 the Conference Board of Canada named Halifax as one of nine so-called hub cities in Canada—cities the federal government should support as engines of regional economic growth. The board, an economic think tank with no real ideological axe to grind, says that when hub cities grow wealthier, their far-flung satellite communities grow wealthier as well. To use the conference board's term, the gap in wealth between rural and urban areas is narrowing because the economy of Halifax is a magnet for wealth, and once the wealth comes to Halifax it radiates outward. Halifax's prosperity is probably the best news on the horizon for the Nova Scotia economy. The *Globe and Mail*'s John Ibbitson wrote, "Canada's future lies in its major cities. Politicians who siphon scarce resources to prop up the hinterlands reduce the wealth of us all, rural and urban alike." Yet there is not a Nova Scotian businessperson or politician from outside Halifax-Dartmouth who subscribes to that view. (Certainly I haven't found one.) The odds are good that any rural politician would not be a politician for long if he or she did make such a statement.

So we need a plan that encourages private sector growth, allows Halifax to flourish, and supports the rural areas. In the next chapter, I hope to outline such a cunning plan.

# *thinking the unthinkable*

*chapter eight*

*F*ormer U.K. prime minister Tony Blair's first cabinet in 1997 included a man named Frank Field, who has since become a bit of an historical footnote. An expert in social policy, Field was appointed minister of welfare. Welfare costs in Britain were spiralling out of control, and Blair wanted him to revamp the system. Blair was widely quoted as having ordered Field to "think the unthinkable" in an imaginative reform of the system. As 1997 progressed, Britons waited for Field's report, and soon grumblings were heard. Chancellor of the Exchequer Gordon Brown was suppressing some of Field's recommendations, said the media, because the minister was proposing higher taxes on the rich to fund programs to help the poor. Such a move would have run counter to Blair and Brown's pledge not to raise taxes. When the report finally emerged it was merely a diluted set of recommendations on welfare fraud. The government could not support Field's original plan. It was unthinkable. Field resigned as a minister after little more than a year in office.

I've thought about Frank Field often while writing this book, not because my recommendations would resemble his in any way. It's just that every time I've written a proposal, I've heard a little voice in the back of my head say, "We can't do that. It would be unthinkable." The problem is we think too much is unthinkable. In the five years since I began writing a column in the *Chronicle Herald*, I've been told the things I wrote were unthinkable. One columnist—a writer I respect—told me my columns were bombastic. If you ever want someone to look at you like you're truly twisted, ask a Nova Scotia politician about privatizing government-owned assets. But as Bernard Goldberg argues in his book, *Arrogance: Rescuing America from the Media Elite*, a love of true diversity means you embrace a diversity of opinion, not just skin colour. So I've tried throughout this book to air views here that some may consider unthinkable, but that we'll be forced to consider because of our circumstances. Will some people disagree with them? I sure hope so. If I can make people think about the unthinkable, to chew it over, debate it, maybe consider how it could be adopted as policy, then I'll consider this book a success.

Consider what I have concluded about Nova Scotia and in many cases the entire Maritimes:

- Per capita take home incomes are at least 10 percent lower than the Canadian average.
- Nova Scotia has the second-oldest population in Canada; it is stagnant and the working population is due to shrink dramatically.
- There are now five working-age citizens for every senior citizen, but that ratio will fall to 2.5-to-1.
- The province has the second-lowest worker productivity in Canada.

- There is no evidence that Nova Scotia is attracting enough immigrants or come-back-from-aways to compensate for what is being lost in outmigration.
- Though Nova Scotians earn less than other Canadians, we pay more for gasoline, most food, home heating, electricity, and other goods and services.
- The province has some of the highest personal and corporate income taxes in Canada, and the government has shown no inclination to lower them.
- The province's harmonized sales tax extends taxation to patches of the service industry that are not taxed in other jurisdictions.
- Property taxes in Halifax are higher than in other municipalities.
- The province has one of the worst records in North America for the start up and survival of small businesses.
- The public sector accounts for 17 percent more of the Nova Scotia economy than the overall Canadian figure, and government has recently been outgrowing private industry.
- Nova Scotia has the oldest infrastructure in the country.
- Nova Scotians are in the bottom four places among Canadian provinces in high school tests in math, science and English.
- Halifax not long ago was the city with the highest crime rate in Canada.
- Nova Scotia is one of four provinces with no universal drug coverage.
- Nova Scotia has the highest death rate among cancer patients in the country.
- Nova Scotia has the fourth-worst record in Canada for producing greenhouse gases from the production of electricity.

- Nova Scotia has the third-highest net debt per capita (and will soon be second as Newfoundland and Labrador pays down its debt).
- Nova Scotia has one of the lowest levels of arts funding in Canada.
- Nova Scotia now gets 40 percent of its provincial government revenue from the federal government, but powerful voices in Central and Western Canada want the equalization program changed.
- There's a 20-percent liability gap in the province's public sector pension plans.
- The Nova Scotia government refuses to promote the Atlantica or TILMA concepts, which aim to increase trade and investment in the region and the northeastern U.S.

Am I arguing that this is a desperate situation and therefore requires desperate measures? No. I don't believe desperate measures are necessary. I'm not calling for extremism. I'm calling for an end to the extremism that Nova Scotia now endures. Yes, extremism. If you plot statistics on economic performance or government spending on a chart for Canada or North America, you will find Nova Scotia occupies extremely poor positions, not the middle of the pack. It's one of the smallest, oldest, most highly taxed, most poorly educated, fiscally dependent, unproductive provinces in Canada. It has the oldest infrastructure and one of the largest public sectors. It exists at the lower extremities of the Canadian experience in a lot of areas, and has to embrace the ideas that can improve this situation.

## New Ideas

Privatization is a shining example. The sale of state-owned assets to the private sector is mainstream policy throughout the socialist European Union, the former Soviet empire, and China. This is a policy that would address some of our biggest problems. The province has too much debt, and it could likely raise five hundred million dollars in four years by selling provincial assets. The private sector accounts for too little of Nova Scotia's economy, and privatization would help improve this situation. What's more, some of the proceeds from privatization could go toward operating costs, which could help to reduce corporate and personal income taxes. Yet, the provincial government has not even considered privatizing wonderful assets like the two bridges over Halifax Harbour or its three hotel resorts. It doesn't make sense.

Some critics would argue—no doubt they will—that this is a right-wing solution. Donald Savoie, the Canada Research Chair in Public Administration at the Université de Moncton, says that we should toss out terms like right wing or left wing and just do what's right. The fact is a pro-business political agenda is now mainstream, and the recession has not changed it. More political experts in our part of the world are recognizing the need for such approaches to solving our problems. This thought occurred to me after I read two documents by Savoie. A native New Brunswicker, Savoie has spent a career in economic development departments in Ottawa, and premier Shawn Graham calls him the world's leading expert on regional economic development. (Nova Scotia premier Darrell Dexter also recently appointed Savoie to a four-member panel on Nova Scotia's future.) In *Visiting Grandchildren: Economic Development in the Maritimes,* Savoie argues that the best solution for the Maritimes would be a full political union, though he believes it's not going to happen in his lifetime. In the absence of Maritime union, Savoie recommends a few steps Ottawa should take to address the Maritimes' economic woes, including reforming employment insurance, moving federal departments to the Maritimes, and paying civil servants less than they would make in Ontario. That solution seemed a bit weak, and maybe Savoie thought so as well, because within a year and a half he had revised and strengthened his conclusions. In a pair of articles for *Progress* magazine in late 2007, Savoie wrote that he wants the Atlantic provinces to adopt market economy policies now prevalent throughout the world. "Our region needs to embrace a business-oriented economic development model, one that, because of its boldness and commitments, will grab the attention of decision-makers everywhere," writes Savoie. "The region should rebrand itself as the place to do business. To do so, policy prescriptions will have to be bold and unambiguous."

To be precise, Savoie boldly and unambiguously prescribes:

- The harmonization, reduction, and possible elimination of corporate income tax across all four Atlantic provinces.
- Spending cuts.
- "A regional rather than provincial perspective on the public sector," which Savoie says will yield opportunities to cut government spending.
- Increasing the minimum wage while reducing social program spending and payments to individuals.
- The transfer of a number of activities to the private sector, including the sale of provincial liquor commissions.
- Reforming the health care sector, including bringing in more private businesses to administer services.

There's not much of a gap between what Savoie has called for and the main themes of this book. I don't think the minimum wage should be raised, not after the recent rise in Nova Scotia. I would also oppose selling off provincial liquor commissions, because there's limited economic gain in privatizing monopolies if they maintain their monopoly status because they still don't experience pricing competition.

Savoie has highlighted the need for spending cuts, and I believe those are essential. There's no way around it: Within a generation, Nova Scotia will have two-and-a-half working citizens for every retiree (there are now five), and the province is starting with a much larger public sector than most others in Canada. Nova Scotia must—absolutely must—reduce the preponderance of government in the economy. The province must at least get to the middle ground in Canada in terms of the public sector as a percentage of the overall economy, and let me emphasize that Canada is a fairly government-friendly country, so achieving the national norm is not calling for a drastic denuding of government. New Brunswick has been leading the way on this movement, and Nova Scotia and P.E.I. need to follow suit. The main goal should be for Nova Scotia to meet the Canadian average for public sector as a proportion of the economy within five years.

## Co-operate and Shrink Government

One group of people who should be actively courted to promote this goal is the civil servants themselves. Yes, it's in their interest to shrink government. Nova Scotia's provincial civil servants, a sizable proportion of who are approaching retirement, are now looking at a $2.5 billion hole in their pension fund. I don't doubt the government will cover some of that gap, but the ability to do so will depend ultimately on the province's economic performance. A shrinking workforce will inevitably lead to a shrinking tax base, and that will restrict the government's ability to meet its pension obligations. A lean government would be in a much better position to cover the pensions than a large government. What's more, the fact that so many civil servants are nearing retirement will make the streamlining of government easier, because the downsizing could be achieved to some degree by retirement rather than by layoffs. These dynamics are at play across the region, and the four provinces have to work together in cutting these costs. If all the business groups and right-wing think tanks have one common piece of advice for the region's governments, it is that they have to work together more closely.

Savoie writes, "A regional rather than a provincial perspective on the public sector and the delivery of public services will yield opportunities to reduce government spending." A careful reading of that sentence shows that Savoie is calling for the three Maritime provinces or four Atlantic provinces to combine departments and agencies to save money. In his *Progress* articles, he notes that a lot of the institutions and health care agencies in the region serve small population bases, and by integrating they could become more efficient. The goal, of course, would be to provide taxpayers with the same level of service while saving taxpayers money. So the main thrust of my recommendation is that Nova Scotia co-operates more with New Brunswick, P.E.I., and Newfoundland and Labrador.

I would not advocate Maritime union, much as I like the concept. It would be too easy for too many special interest groups to entangle the process with side issues and nothing would change. We need the benefits of co-operation soon, given that the demographic demons are staring us in the face. There's already a realization in governments in all the provinces that we need to work together more. Darrell Dexter said plainly, in our interview while he was still acclimatizing himself to the premier's office, that he was open to co-operating with other provinces, and New Brunswick's Shawn Graham told me it was "critical" that the provinces co-operate more. But the devil will be in the details. The Atlantic premiers historically have got along like four cats in a pillowcase and are more inclined to share poverty than to see one province get ahead of the others. That attitude has to be replaced with the correct perception that a development that helps one place in Atlantic Canada helps all of Atlantic Canada.

Overall, we need to satisfy at least one of three goals when we co-operate with our neighbours: first, increase the money flowing into the region; second, reduce the size of government; and third, reduce the fragmentation of the four tiny economies. These will be difficult to meet because we sometimes have different interests, and because co-operation or consolidation can actually increase costs rather than cut them. Consider Halifax Regional Municipality or the European Union. Ideally, when organizations merge, they keep the best parts of the amalgamating groups and toss away what they don't need. It's a painful process, given that usually what's tossed away is employees. I'm not going to understate the upheaval this can cause in families whose breadwinners lose their jobs. But the laid off people eventually find other jobs, and the organizations brought together can thrive as an enlarged group that has inherited the best parts of the original compo-nents. Unfortunately, in public sector mergers, mass layoffs are too often politically unthinkable. So the overseers tend to let everyone keep their jobs, then hire a new layer of bureaucracy to oversee the enlarged group. Though it seems more humane than huge layoffs, it undoubtedly defeats the purpose of merging.

I can speak about this with a bit of authority, because my main job for the past decade has been reporting for *The Deal*, a New York-based publication that focuses on mergers and acquisitions. In this capacity, I once had a fascinating interview with Ken Harvey, the chief technology officer for the global bank HSBC Holdings plc, at the company's head-quarters in London's Docklands. Harvey is an American who joined HSBC when the bank bought consumer finance company Household

International Inc. of Prospect Heights, Illinois, for $14.6 billion (U.S.) in 2003. The deal turned out to be disastrous, because it exposed the bank to the U.S. mortgage market. When HSBC bought Household, it brought on Harvey to run the IT department, and when HSBC in turn bought Bank of Bermuda in 2005, the buyer decided that the Bermudan bank had the better IT global fund services platform. Though Bank of Bermuda was 1 percent the size of HSBC, the buyer ended up tossing out its fund services platform and adopting that of the Bermuda bank. "I would like to think that our system is the repository of the best systems of all the institutions that we've bought," Harvey told me.

Could we construct a bureaucracy in the Maritimes or the Atlantic provinces that is the repository of the best components of the three or four governments in the region? It's nice to think that we could, though there's no reason for optimism. Who would be in charge of such talks? The Council of Atlantic Premiers is effectively ineffective, to put it politely and oxymoronically. The governments like to hold up the Atlantic Lottery Corporation as an example of pan-regional co-operation, but it really just operates a monopoly that panders to people's proclivity to gamble. Meanwhile, I could point to the failed overtures New Brunswick has made in combining our pension plans as evidence that we cannot co-operate and build effective pan-regional institutions.

There is one institution that gives me hope that the four Atlantic provinces can co-operate. It's often held up to ridicule by conservatives, but it has grown in stature and proven its longevity. It is the Atlantic Canada Opportunities Agency (ACOA), and I think it represents our best chance for getting the eastern provinces to work together. ACOA is not a body that just hands out money to politically connected busi-nesspeople. ACOA has become the federal government's voice in the region, and it has adopted a diplomatic as well as a developmental role.

It acts as a referee between the provinces, helping to strike agreements between the bickering parties. It has the power to impose order on the four provinces because to varying degrees they all need the federal government for financial aid. At least twice it has shown itself to be an effective herder of Atlantic Canadian cats. It chaired the negotiations for the Atlantic Gateway in 2007–2008. These talks began as a federal-provincial program to develop infrastructure so the region could boast coordinated air, sea, rail, and road transport links to the outside world. The concept was first proposed by the Port of Halifax and other Halifax business groups, and soon erupted into an interprovincial spat in which everyone tried to get their paws on federal money. "So far, most people have focused on Halifax, on containers," Newfoundland and Labrador Transport Minister Trevor Taylor told me in an interview, summing up the views of all participants outside Halifax. "It's not to the other three provinces' advantage to have all the money in the region spent in Halifax." Late in 2007, Peter MacKay, the minister responsible for ACOA, had the four provinces strike a committee to hash out who should get what in the Gateway funding. The committee was chaired by ACOA, and by the end of 2008 it had agreed what money should be given to whom and for what. It would be difficult to argue that the money created a harmonized, intermodal transportation network, as was the original intent. But everyone went away happy.

In March 2009, MacKay made another announcement with the word "Gateway" in the headline, when he unveiled the Atlantic Energy Gateway. Again, ACOA has been asked to play the role of Jimmy Carter among the combatants, and I bet it will come up with a messy solution that will satisfy, if not thrill, all the players. It's essential that ACOA's mandate be enlarged. I came to this conclusion after an interview with Leanne Hachey of the CFIB, when we were discussing the need to reduce government spending in the region. She said the four provinces had to combine services, and that it may even reach the point at which the federal government should withhold transfer payments unless the Atlantic provinces combine departments. She said it could be done through the Council of Atlantic Premiers, without extra costs.

I agree with all she said except about the council of premiers. I think the four governments are genetically incapable of sitting down and saying, "We all have to cut costs, so let's all combine certain departments and headquarter them among the four provinces." It's just not going to happen. Because of its resource wealth, Newfoundland is suddenly the most successful. New Brunswick is singular in its reformist mindset. All are fighting to boost their rural economies, and parts of all provinces harbour incredible resentment of Halifax. If the premiers were left to themselves to negotiate a deal, I doubt they would reach an agreement. But I believe the federal government could get the four provinces to agree conceptually on the need for rationalized services, and sign up to a committee headed by ACOA to work out a method to consolidate some provincial departments.

If you ask me—and I realize no one other than my editor has—these negotiations will need significant arm-twisting, moral suasion, and some threats. Only the federal government can get results in this area, and the best federal agency to do it is ACOA. MacKay should strike another committee—one on consolidation of provincial agencies—and give ACOA the job of selecting provincial agencies whose work could be expanded to the whole region. This should not be optional. Ottawa should let the four provinces know that if they want to continue to receive so much of their revenue from Ottawa, they are going to have to rationalize the expenditure. If these warnings become public, they will no doubt spark resentment in Atlantic Canada (which has 32 seats in the House of Commons) and overwhelming applause in the rest of Canada (250 seats). Do the math and tell me this isn't a winning strategy for Ottawa. The federal government hands about eight billion dollars a year to the Atlantic provinces. It has an interest in imposing reforms on us—especially ones that will help our economy.

Again, the best institutions should survive. For example, the New Brunswick Investment Management Corporation should manage the pensions of all four provinces. Maybe it could have an alternative investment division based in Prince Edward Island to oversee venture capital, private equity, and infrastructure investments with a portion of the pension funds. InNOVAcorp could expand its mentoring and VC work to encompass young businesses throughout the region. The Newfoundland and Labrador tourism department could lend their tourism expertise to the whole region. The end result would be to expand the agency that is regarded as the best in the region, and shut down the others. Just like the HSBC information technology department, we'll keep what's best and discard the remainder. After that, we could gear up the program to consolidate other agencies and departments.

As the program takes hold, another dimension should be added to it. We should allow municipalities throughout the region to compete to be headquarters of the various agencies and departments. This is a major plank in my platform because it solves two problems. First, and most important, we have to do something to alleviate rural decline, and second, we have to ease the resentment against Halifax. Halifax has to be allowed to grow as the business and academic hub of the region, and in return it has to surrender some of the public sector institutions it now hosts. As we have seen previously, there is a growing consensus that regions need hub cities to grow, and the wealth from these hubs radiates outward. That's the theory, and I subscribe to the theory. The main problem is how long wealth takes to flow down the spokes. My best guess is it would take, say, a decade for the increasing wealth of Halifax (and St. John's and Saint John) to spill out to other areas. In the meantime the outlying areas are struggling with declining population, shrinking tax bases, and growing unemployment. Does anyone expect citizens of rural communities to buy into the hub theory of development under these circumstances?

The overall result of the consolidation of government services should move government offices into outlying areas. People I have discussed this with have expressed concern the result will be an overall reduction in government efficiency, but I don't buy it. We live in an age of telecommuting and governments should be able to operate with satellite bureaucracies without increasing costs. There is no way the administrative costs of having rural government offices would exceed the economic and human costs of allowing further declines in small and medium-sized towns, not to mention industrial Cape Breton. Rural bureaucracy will reduce the amount of money we have to devote to futile projects that prop up the small towns.

As the program develops, the provinces should examine a unified health department. This would obviously be one of the biggest catches for any municipality, and its headquarters should be located in a medium-sized city, possibly in Sydney, Charlottetown, Corner Brook, or northern New Brunswick. Other provinces could develop into centres of excellence in specific disciplines, probably located in the Moncton-Amherst-Summerside area so they have ready contact with each other. Should education retain three separate departments? Probably. Each province has certain areas it wishes to stress in education. But the Nova Scotia government should fight the fight to do away with its own school board structure. The school boards have failed to develop a high standard of education—even a moderate standard—and they should be abolished and education centralized in the provincial education department. The cost savings would be substantial and could be applied to teachers and classroom resources.

In the spirit of reinvigorating depressed areas, the Nova Scotia government should strike a committee to study two measures that could support urban Cape Breton. We have come to the point at which senior civil servants in CBRM are discussing a split from Nova Scotia. We're not talking about a loony fringe group, but the senior people at the heart of government in Cape Breton. The warning bells are sounding. There's a crisis brewing in Cape Breton and we need to do something big to assist the island. The provincial government ought to consider either moving several departments to Sydney or asking the federal government to move Maritime Command to the Sydney area. Sydney has a deepwater port, is close to Europe, and has all the amenities that the military would need. It would be an economic godsend for Cape Breton, and after the initial shock of the move the military families would no doubt love Cape Breton as much as the people who now live there. The move would have the added benefit of freeing up prime commercial real estate in Halifax, allowing for the expansion of the downtown. Failing that, several large departments, such as Health or Education, should move to Sydney. Halifax does not need government employment, but Sydney badly does. It would be a bold move. Is it unthinkable? I hope not.

The other side of this proposal is to encourage the growth of Halifax as the private sector's administrative headquarters. We need to grow the private sector, and most private sector companies want to grow in Halifax because the city offers more human resources than other parts of the province or region. The government should not favour businesses that want to settle or expand in Halifax rather than other regions, but it should not give more subsidies to enterprises targeting rural areas either. Universities in Halifax should merge, and become a singe centre of excellence for research. Then the business-generation capabilities of InNOVAcorp can help commercialize that research, and the knowledge economy could blossom. Let Halifax thrive, and over time the region will benefit.

This vision is hardly unthinkable. It is really quite simple. We should merge government departments and agencies between the provinces and within the province, aiming even to have a single health department. The savings should be used first to lower personal and corporate income tax, and then to pay down the debt. Our aim should be to rationally reduce the size of government without compromising services and to increase the private sector. We should seek to enhance Halifax's position as the commercial centre of Atlantic Canada, and encourage this development by moving government offices to smaller centres. Provincial assets should be privatized. Government pension funds should back alternative investments. As I've mentioned earlier, these proposals should go hand-in-hand with policies of privatization, a TILMA, promotion of Atlantica, lower taxes, expansion of NSBI and InNOVAcorp, and the elimination of the industrial expansion fund.

None of these measures would cure the demographic juggernaut that our new premier warns of. But taken together, they should build a more competitive economy, which would help to attract more people to the region. We already have a head start in attracting people because this is such a pleasant place to live, but without economic improvements we're going to continue to bleed young people. We will, in short, become an economic backwater.